EXPLORING INTERNET JOURNALISM

Navigating the Digital Frontier

EXPLORING INTERNET JOURNALISM

OSMAN KARAKAS

About Book

Book Title: Exploring Internet Journalism: Navigating the Digital Frontier

Format: Word/PDF

Size: 6X9 inches - 15.24X22.89 cm

Total Pages: 203

E-mail: okarakas@hotmail.com

Web: www.osmankarakas.com

CONTENTS

Preface:

Welcome to the world of Internet Journalism, a field where the digital age has not only revolutionized the way news is reported and consumed but has also empowered individuals and communities to participate in the creation of news. In this book, we embark on a journey through the dynamic landscape of online journalism, exploring its evolution, ethical challenges, tools and technologies, and the boundless opportunities it offers to storytellers and truth-seekers in the digital era.

The internet has brought about a seismic shift in the way information is disseminated. It has dismantled the traditional barriers to entry, enabling anyone with an internet connection and a voice to become a news source. While this democratization of news has enriched the global conversation, it has also given rise to concerns about the spread of misinformation and the erosion of trust in journalism. As we delve into these complex issues, we also discover the resilience of journalistic values and the commitment of internet journalists to uphold the principles of accuracy, fairness, and transparency.

Our exploration takes us through the evolving role of technology in journalism, from data-driven reporting to multimedia storytelling, and the critical importance of search engine optimization (SEO) in reaching wider audiences. We dive into the world of social media and the power it wields in news dissemination and audience engagement. We examine the ethical dilemmas internet journalists face in the age of viral content and fake news, and we learn how they navigate these challenges while maintaining their integrity.

As we traverse the chapters of this book, you will find practical guidance for aspiring internet journalists, from building a strong online presence to networking and collaborating in the digital space. We also delve into case studies, highlighting successful online news stories and lessons learned from high-impact internet journalism. Along the way, we explore the common mistakes to avoid in online reporting and offer tips for aspiring journalists to thrive in this rapidly evolving field.

We believe that internet journalism, at its core, is about storytelling and information sharing. It's about amplifying voices, uncovering truths, and engaging with audiences in ways that were unimaginable just a few decades ago. Whether you're an aspiring journalist, a seasoned professional, or simply a curious reader, this book invites you to delve into the exciting world of internet journalism, where innovation meets tradition, and the pursuit of truth remains at the heart of the digital revolution.

We hope you find this book to be an insightful and valuable resource as you navigate the ever-changing landscape of internet journalism. It's a journey filled with challenges and opportunities, and we invite you to embark on it with an open mind and a commitment to journalistic integrity. Together, we'll explore the past, present, and future of internet journalism and the transformative power it holds.

Thank you for joining us on this exploration of Internet Journalism, and we look forward to the stories you'll uncover and the impact you'll make in this dynamic field.

Osman Karakas

Author

Journalist & Lecturer & Publisher

Chapter 1: Introduction to Internet Journalism

Defining Internet Journalism

In the ever-evolving landscape of journalism, the digital age has ushered in a transformative era that is reshaping the way news is produced, disseminated, and consumed. Internet journalism, often referred to as online journalism or digital journalism, stands at the forefront of this revolution. It is a dynamic and multifaceted field that combines traditional journalism principles with cutting-edge technology to deliver news and information to a global audience like never before.

The Digital Revolution

To truly understand the essence of Internet journalism, we must first acknowledge the seismic shifts that have taken place in the world of media and communication. The advent of the internet has dismantled the barriers that once confined news reporting to print publications, television broadcasts, and radio waves. Today, anyone with a smartphone or computer can access news from around the world in real-time. This democratization of information has given rise to a new breed of journalists, unbound by the constraints of traditional media.

What Is Internet Journalism?

Internet journalism encompasses a vast spectrum of activities related to the creation and distribution of news and information through digital channels. At its core, it involves the use of online platforms, websites, social media, and multimedia tools to report, analyze, and present news stories to an online audience. Internet journalists leverage the power of the internet to reach a global readership, engage with their audience, and provide timely updates on evolving stories.

Key Elements of Internet Journalism

1. Multimedia Integration

Internet journalism embraces the use of multimedia elements to enhance storytelling. This includes embedding images, videos, audio clips, infographics, and interactive features within news articles to provide a richer and more engaging experience for readers.

2. Real-time Reporting

In the digital age, news unfolds at a rapid pace. Internet journalists are expected to provide real-time updates and live coverage of breaking news events. This immediacy sets online journalism apart from traditional forms of reporting.

3. Audience Engagement

Unlike the one-way communication of traditional media, internet journalism fosters two-way interaction with the audience. Readers can comment on articles, share their perspectives on social media, and even contribute to the news through user-generated content.

4. Data-driven Insights

Data journalism has become a hallmark of internet journalism. Journalists mine and analyze data to uncover trends, patterns, and stories that may have otherwise remained hidden. Data visualizations are commonly used to make complex information more accessible to readers.

The Changing Role of Journalists

As we delve deeper into the world of internet journalism, it becomes evident that the role of journalists has evolved significantly. Internet journalists are not just reporters; they are curators, fact-checkers, community builders, and multimedia storytellers. They navigate the vast digital landscape, verifying information, debunking falsehoods, and providing context to the news.

The Global Reach

One of the most remarkable aspects of internet journalism is its ability to transcend geographical boundaries. A news story published by an internet journalist in one corner of the world can be read, shared, and discussed by individuals on the opposite side of the globe within seconds. This global reach amplifies the impact of journalism, making it a potent force for change and awareness.

Conclusion

In this introductory chapter, we have scratched the surface of the fascinating world of internet journalism.

As we progress through this book, we will delve deeper into the various facets of online journalism, exploring the tools, techniques, and ethical considerations that define this dynamic field. Internet journalism is more than just a medium; it is a conduit for information, a platform for storytelling, and a catalyst for the future of journalism.

In the chapters that follow, we will explore the structure of a digital newsroom, delve into the ethical challenges that internet journalists face, and learn how to craft compelling content for the web. Additionally, we will examine the role of multimedia, the impact of social media, and the exciting possibilities of data journalism. Through case studies, practical tips, and real-world examples, we will equip you with the knowledge and skills to thrive in the realm of internet journalism.

So, let's embark on this journey into the heart of online journalism, where words, images, and ideas flow seamlessly through the digital channels that connect us all.

Evolution of Journalism in the Digital Age

The history of journalism is a story of adaptation, innovation, and transformation. From its earliest origins as handwritten newsletters in the 17th century to the globally interconnected digital landscape of today, journalism has constantly evolved to meet the changing needs and expectations of its audience. In this chapter, we embark on a journey through time to explore the remarkable evolution of journalism in the digital age.

The Print Era: Journalism's Birth

Journalism, in its nascent form, emerged during the Enlightenment era in the 17th century. The invention of the printing press by Johannes Gutenberg revolutionized the dissemination of information. Newspapers and magazines began to proliferate, offering a medium through which news, opinions, and information could be shared with a broader audience. The print era was characterized by the physical production of newspapers, which were delivered to homes and newsstands.

The Broadcast Era: Radio and Television

The 20th century witnessed the rise of radio and television as powerful mediums for journalism. Radio broadcasts delivered news updates directly to people's homes, making it the go-to source for breaking news during events like World War II. Television further revolutionized journalism with its ability to provide visual coverage of events. The evening news became a staple in American households, and news anchors like Walter Cronkite achieved iconic status.

The Digital Revolution

The turning point in journalism's evolution came with the advent of the internet. The digital revolution disrupted traditional news models and paved the way for internet journalism. In the 1990s, news websites began to emerge, offering a new way for readers to access information online. This marked the beginning of a seismic shift that would forever change the media landscape.

Birth of Internet Journalism

Internet journalism, also known as online journalism or digital journalism, emerged as a response to the internet's transformative capabilities. News organizations adapted to the digital age by creating websites, where they could publish articles, videos, and multimedia content. The internet opened up new avenues for reporting, allowing journalists to reach global audiences instantly.

Characteristics of Internet Journalism

Internet journalism is characterized by several key features:

1. Real-time Updates

The digital nature of internet journalism enables real-time reporting and updates. Journalists can publish breaking news within minutes of an event occurring, keeping audiences informed as events unfold.

2. Multimedia Integration

Internet journalism embraces multimedia elements, including images, videos, infographics, and interactive content. This enriches the storytelling experience and engages readers more effectively.

3. Audience Interaction

Unlike traditional media, internet journalism encourages two-way communication. Readers can comment on articles, share content on social media, and even contribute their own perspectives and content.

4. Global Reach

The internet knows no geographical boundaries. Internet journalism allows news to be instantly accessible to a global audience, transcending traditional limitations.

The Changing Role of Journalists

As journalism evolved into the digital age, so did the role of journalists. Internet journalists are not mere conveyors of information; they are curators, fact-checkers, community builders, and multimedia storytellers. They navigate the vast digital landscape, verifying information, debunking falsehoods, and providing context to the news.

Conclusion

In this introductory chapter, we've traced the fascinating journey of journalism from its print origins to its current state in the digital age. As we continue through this book, we'll delve deeper into the nuances of internet journalism, exploring the tools, techniques, and ethical considerations that define this dynamic field. Internet journalism is more than just a medium; it is a conduit for information, a platform for storytelling, and a catalyst for the future of journalism.

In the chapters that follow, we'll explore the structure of a digital newsroom, navigate the ethical challenges that internet journalists face, and learn how to craft compelling content for the web. We'll also delve into the role of multimedia, the impact of social media, and the exciting possibilities of data journalism. Through case studies, practical tips, and real-world examples, we aim to equip you with the knowledge and skills to thrive in the realm of internet journalism.

The Importance of Internet Journalism

In today's fast-paced and interconnected world, the significance of Internet journalism cannot be overstated. As we embark on this journey through the realm of online journalism, it's crucial to understand why this field holds a pivotal role in shaping our information landscape and influencing our society.

A Global Information Network

The internet has transformed the way we access and consume information. It has broken down geographical barriers, enabling news and stories to travel across the globe in a matter of seconds. Internet journalism leverages this global information network to disseminate news, making it accessible to a diverse and international audience.

Timely and Relevant Updates

One of the fundamental aspects that sets internet journalism apart is its ability to provide timely and relevant updates. In a world where news unfolds rapidly, internet journalists can publish breaking news, analysis, and feature stories with unprecedented speed. This immediacy is invaluable in keeping the public informed about unfolding events.

Diverse Perspectives and Voices

Internet journalism has opened the door to a multitude of voices and perspectives. Online platforms provide a space for diverse communities and underrepresented voices to share their stories and viewpoints. This diversity enriches the information landscape and fosters a more inclusive and informed society.

Holding Power Accountable

Journalism has long played a crucial role in holding those in power accountable for their actions. Internet journalism takes this responsibility to new heights by providing a platform for investigative reporting, fact-checking, and uncovering hidden truths. It empowers citizens with the information they need to make informed decisions and demand transparency from their leaders.

Bridging the Gap

Internet journalism also serves as a bridge between traditional media and the digital age. Established news organizations have adapted to the digital landscape, reaching audiences through websites, social media, podcasts, and interactive content. This transition ensures that the principles of journalism—accuracy, fairness, and objectivity—are maintained in the digital realm.

Engaging the Audience

In the digital era, audience engagement is paramount. Internet journalism fosters two-way communication, allowing readers to participate in discussions, offer feedback, and share content. This engagement not only strengthens the bond between journalists and their audience but also helps in the collective pursuit of truth.

Navigating the Information Deluge

The internet is a vast sea of information, and navigating it can be overwhelming. Internet journalism plays a critical role in curating, verifying, and contextualizing information. Journalists sift through the deluge of data to present readers with credible and meaningful stories.

Adapting to Change

In a rapidly changing media landscape, internet journalism embodies adaptability. It embraces emerging technologies, storytelling formats, and distribution channels. Journalists in this field are at the forefront of innovation, exploring new ways to engage with their audience and convey complex information.

Conclusion

As we embark on this exploration of internet journalism, we must recognize its vital role in our modern society. Internet journalism is not just a medium for reporting news; it is a powerful force that shapes public opinion, fosters accountability, and connects individuals across borders. It represents the future of journalism, where the fusion of traditional values and digital innovation paves the way for a more informed and interconnected world.

In the chapters that follow, we will delve into the practical aspects of internet journalism, from the structure of digital newsrooms to the ethical considerations that guide online reporting. We will explore the tools, techniques, and case studies that illustrate the diverse and dynamic nature of this field. Together, we will journey through the evolving landscape of internet journalism and discover the opportunities and challenges it presents.

Chapter 2: The Digital Newsroom

The Structure of a Digital Newsroom

The heart of effective internet journalism lies within the digital newsroom—a dynamic and collaborative space where journalists, editors, and multimedia professionals come together to craft and disseminate news stories to a global audience. In this section, we will explore the essential components and roles within a digital newsroom.

1. Editors and Managing Editors

Editors are the backbone of a digital newsroom. They oversee the editorial process, ensuring that stories are accurate, well-written, and aligned with the publication's guidelines. Managing editors coordinate the efforts of the editorial team, assign stories, and make critical decisions about what news to cover. They play a pivotal role in maintaining the quality and integrity of the publication.

2. Reporters and Correspondents

Reporters and correspondents are the journalists on the ground. They gather information through research, interviews, and firsthand reporting. In the digital age, reporters often need to be versatile, capable of producing written articles, audio reports, video segments, and multimedia content. Their work forms the foundation of news stories.

3. Photojournalists and Videographers

Visual storytelling is a cornerstone of internet journalism. Photojournalists and videographers capture compelling images and footage to complement news stories. They are skilled in photography, video production, and editing, adding depth and context to reporting.

4. Multimedia Producers

Multimedia producers specialize in creating interactive and engaging content. They develop multimedia elements such as infographics, interactive graphics, and data visualizations. These assets enhance the reader's understanding of complex topics and make stories more immersive.

5. Web Developers and Designers

The presentation of news on digital platforms is the responsibility of web developers and designers. They ensure that the publication's website is user-friendly, visually appealing, and responsive on various devices. Web developers also handle technical aspects like content management systems (CMS) and site maintenance.

6. Social Media Managers

In the age of social media, reaching the audience extends beyond the website. Social media managers are responsible for curating and sharing news on platforms like Twitter, Facebook, Instagram, and LinkedIn. They engage with the audience, promote stories, and monitor feedback and discussions.

7. Data Analysts and Visualization Specialists

Data journalism has become a cornerstone of digital reporting. Data analysts and visualization specialists work with large datasets to uncover trends and insights. They create data-driven stories, interactive charts, and infographics to make complex information more accessible to readers.

8. Audience Engagement Editors

Audience engagement editors focus on building and nurturing a community around the publication. They encourage reader participation through comments, discussions, and user-generated content. These editors facilitate dialogue and ensure the publication is responsive to its audience.

9. Content Managers and SEO Specialists

Content managers oversee the organization and publication of articles. They work closely with SEO specialists to optimize content for search engines, ensuring that news stories reach a wider online audience. Their efforts contribute to the visibility and discoverability of the publication.

10. Legal and Ethical Advisors

In the digital newsroom, legal and ethical advisors play a critical role in ensuring that stories are legally sound and adhere to ethical standards. They provide guidance on issues related to libel, privacy, copyright, and conflicts of interest, helping journalists navigate potential pitfalls.

11. Audience Analytics and Metrics Analysts

Understanding the impact of news stories is essential. Audience analytics and metrics analysts track the performance of content, analyzing metrics such as page views, engagement rates, and audience demographics. This data informs editorial decisions and helps measure the effectiveness of reporting.

In the digital newsroom, these roles collaborate closely, often in real-time, to produce and deliver news stories to a global audience. The structure of a digital newsroom is adaptable and responsive to the ever-changing demands of online journalism. It thrives on creativity, innovation, and a commitment to upholding the principles of journalistic integrity.

In the following chapters, we will delve deeper into the functions and challenges faced by each role within the digital newsroom. We will explore how effective collaboration among these professionals leads to the creation of compelling and impactful news stories.

Roles and Responsibilities in Online Journalism

In the fast-paced world of online journalism, each member of the newsroom plays a unique and vital role in delivering timely, accurate, and engaging news to a global audience. Understanding these roles and their respective responsibilities is essential for effective collaboration and the successful creation of compelling news content.

1. Editors and Managing Editors
- Assigning and prioritizing news stories.
- Ensuring editorial guidelines and standards are maintained.
- Reviewing and editing content for accuracy, clarity, and style.
- Making decisions on story placement and prominence.

2. Reporters and Correspondents
- Conducting research and interviews to gather news.
- Writing articles, reports, and news updates.
- Verifying information and fact-checking.
- Adapting to various formats, including written, audio, and video reporting.

3. Photojournalists and Videographers
- Capturing compelling images and video footage.
- Editing and enhancing visual content.
- Collaborating with reporters to provide visual context for stories.
- Ensuring high-quality multimedia elements.

4. Multimedia Producers
- Creating interactive and engaging multimedia content.

- Developing infographics, data visualizations, and interactive graphics.
- Enhancing storytelling through multimedia elements.
- Ensuring compatibility with various devices and platforms.

5. Web Developers and Designers

- Designing and maintaining the publication's website.
- Ensuring a user-friendly and responsive web design.
- Implementing technical solutions and content management systems.
- Optimizing website performance and security.

6. Social Media Managers

- Curating and sharing news content on social media platforms.
- Engaging with the audience through comments and discussions.
- Monitoring social media trends and feedback.
- Promoting the publication and increasing its social media presence.

7. Data Analysts and Visualization Specialists

- Analyzing large datasets to identify trends and insights.
- Creating data-driven stories, charts, and infographics.
- Ensuring accuracy and integrity in data reporting.
- Visualizing complex information for reader comprehension.

8. Audience Engagement Editors

- Facilitating reader participation through comments and discussions.
- Encouraging user-generated content and contributions.
- Fostering a sense of community around the publication.
- Responding to reader inquiries and feedback.

9. Content Managers and SEO Specialists

- Organizing and scheduling content publication.
- Collaborating with SEO specialists to optimize content for search engines.
- Managing the publication's content archive.
- Ensuring content alignment with editorial strategy.

10. Legal and Ethical Advisors

- Providing guidance on legal and ethical issues in journalism.

- Reviewing content for potential libel, privacy violations, or copyright concerns.

- Advising on conflicts of interest and ethical decision-making.

- Ensuring adherence to journalistic principles and legal standards.

11. Audience Analytics and Metrics Analysts

- *Monitoring and analyzing audience engagement metrics.*
- *Evaluating the performance of news stories and content.*
- *Generating insights to inform editorial decisions.*
- *Reporting on audience demographics and behavior.*

These roles are interdependent, and effective communication and collaboration among team members are essential for producing high-quality news content in the digital newsroom. In the following chapters, we will delve deeper into each role, exploring their challenges, best practices, and how they contribute to the creation of informative and engaging news stories.

Tools and Technologies for Internet Journalism

In the ever-evolving landscape of online journalism, staying up-to-date with the latest tools and technologies is essential. Journalists and media professionals rely on a variety of digital tools to streamline their work, enhance storytelling, and engage with audiences. Here, we'll explore some of the essential tools and technologies that power internet journalism.

Content Management Systems (CMS)

Content Management Systems are the backbone of digital newsrooms. They provide a platform for publishing, organizing, and managing content on websites. Common CMS platforms include WordPress, Drupal, and Joomla. These systems enable editors, reporters, and content managers to publish articles, images, videos, and multimedia elements seamlessly.

Digital Audio Workstations (DAWs)

For audio journalism and podcasting, Digital Audio Workstations are indispensable. Software like Adobe Audition, Audacity, and GarageBand allows journalists to record, edit, and produce high-quality audio content. DAWs are essential for creating podcasts, audio reports, and interviews.

Video Editing Software

Video is a powerful storytelling medium, and video editing software is a vital tool for multimedia journalists. Tools like Adobe Premiere Pro, Final Cut Pro, and DaVinci Resolve enable professionals to edit, enhance, and produce video content for online news platforms.

Data Visualization Tools

Data journalism relies on data visualization tools to make complex information accessible. Tools such as Tableau, D3.js, and Infogram allow journalists to create interactive charts, maps, and infographics. These visualizations enhance the storytelling process and provide readers with a deeper understanding of data-driven stories.

Social Media Management Platforms

Social media plays a crucial role in news distribution and audience engagement. Social media management platforms like Hootsuite, Buffer, and Sprout Social enable newsrooms to schedule posts, track engagement metrics, and manage multiple social media accounts efficiently.

Analytics and Tracking Tools

Understanding audience behavior and content performance is vital in internet journalism. Tools like Google Analytics, Chartbeat, and Parse.ly provide insights into web traffic, user engagement, and audience demographics. Journalists use these analytics to optimize content strategies.

Collaboration and Communication Tools

Effective communication and collaboration are essential in digital newsrooms. Tools such as Slack, Microsoft Teams, and Trello facilitate real-time communication, file sharing, project management, and task coordination among team members.

Mobile Journalism (MoJo) Apps

Mobile journalism apps empower journalists to report from the field using smartphones and tablets. Apps like FiLMiC Pro, Adobe Premiere Rush, and iMovie enable mobile reporting, live streaming, and on-the-go video editing.

Search Engine Optimization (SEO) Tools

SEO is crucial for online visibility. SEO tools like Moz, SEMrush, and Ahrefs help journalists optimize content for search engines. This ensures that news stories rank well in search results and reach a broader online audience.

Secure Communication and Encryption Tools

Protecting sources and sensitive information is paramount in journalism. Secure communication tools like Signal and encryption tools like VeraCrypt provide a secure means of exchanging confidential information while safeguarding privacy.

Content Distribution Platforms

Content distribution platforms like Outbrain and Taboola help news organizations reach a wider audience by recommending their content on other websites. These platforms promote articles, videos, and multimedia content to relevant readers.

Virtual Reality (VR) and Augmented Reality (AR) Tools

Emerging technologies like VR and AR are transforming storytelling. Tools like Adobe Aero and Unity enable journalists to create immersive experiences, allowing readers to interact with news stories in three dimensions.

These tools and technologies are integral to the modern digital newsroom, enhancing the efficiency and capabilities of journalists and content creators. Embracing innovation and staying informed about the latest advancements in internet journalism tools is crucial for delivering engaging and impactful news in the digital age.

In the following chapters, we will explore how these tools are used in practical newsroom settings and how they contribute to the creation of compelling internet journalism.

Chapter 3: Ethics and Credibility in Internet Journalism

Ethical Challenges in Online Reporting

As internet journalism continues to evolve, journalists face a unique set of ethical challenges in the digital realm. Navigating these challenges is crucial to maintaining credibility and trust with the audience. In this section, we'll delve into some of the prominent ethical dilemmas that online reporters encounter:

1. Accuracy in a Fast-Paced Environment

In the digital age, news spreads at lightning speed. Journalists often face pressure to be the first to break a story. This urgency can lead to errors, as facts may be misinterpreted or insufficiently verified. Maintaining accuracy in a fast-paced environment is a significant challenge, and journalists must strike a balance between speed and precision.

2. Verification of User-Generated Content

User-generated content, including photos and videos shared on social media, has become a valuable source of news. However, verifying the authenticity and context of such content can be challenging. Journalists must exercise caution and employ verification techniques to ensure the accuracy of user-contributed material.

3. Balancing Sensationalism and Sensitivity

Sensationalism can drive online engagement, but it often comes at the expense of sensitivity and ethical reporting. Journalists must grapple with the ethical dilemma of when and how to report on sensitive topics, such as tragedy or violence, without resorting to sensationalism that can exploit the suffering of individuals or communities.

4. Transparency in Sponsored Content

Many online news outlets rely on sponsored content and native advertising to generate revenue. Maintaining transparency and clearly distinguishing between editorial content and sponsored material is essential to avoid misleading readers. Journalists must uphold the principle of transparency and clearly label sponsored content.

5. Handling Online Harassment and Trolling

Online journalists are susceptible to harassment and trolling from readers and internet users. Responding to online abuse while maintaining professionalism and ethical conduct can be challenging. Journalists must establish boundaries for engagement and know when to disengage from harmful interactions.

6. Privacy and Surveillance Concerns

Reporting on topics related to privacy and surveillance raises ethical questions about the potential harm caused by disclosing sensitive information. Journalists must weigh the public's right to know against the potential invasion of individuals' privacy, especially when reporting on topics like government surveillance or data breaches.

7. Ethical Use of User Data

Online news organizations often collect user data to tailor content and advertising. Ethical considerations regarding data privacy, consent, and transparency are critical. Journalists and news organizations must handle user data responsibly and comply with relevant data protection regulations.

8. Avoiding Plagiarism and Attribution

In the digital age, information is easily accessible, which can lead to plagiarism or inadequate attribution of sources. Journalists must uphold ethical standards by providing proper attribution for sources and original reporting. Plagiarism damages credibility and can have legal consequences.

9. Conflict of Interest in Digital Media

Journalists in online media may face conflicts of interest related to their personal affiliations or financial interests. Full disclosure of conflicts of interest is essential to maintain transparency and uphold journalistic integrity. Journalists must be vigilant in avoiding situations that compromise their independence.

10. Responsible Social Media Use

Journalists' personal use of social media can impact their professional image. Ethical guidelines for responsible social media use, including avoiding biased or offensive content, are crucial. Journalists must be aware that their online presence reflects on their news organization.

Addressing these ethical challenges in online reporting requires a commitment to ethical principles, transparency, and ongoing education. Journalists must adhere to their news organization's code of ethics and seek guidance when facing complex ethical dilemmas. By upholding high ethical standards, online journalists can maintain the trust of their readers and contribute to the credibility of internet journalism as a whole.

In the subsequent chapters, we will explore ethical guidelines and best practices that journalists can employ to navigate these challenges effectively.

This section provides a detailed examination of the ethical challenges that online reporters encounter, emphasizing the importance of ethical conduct in maintaining credibility and trust in internet journalism.

Maintaining Credibility and Trust

Credibility and trust are the cornerstones of effective journalism, especially in the digital age where misinformation and disinformation can spread rapidly. Internet journalists must be vigilant in upholding their credibility and fostering trust with their audience. Here are key strategies for maintaining credibility and trust in online reporting:

1. Adhere to Ethical Standards

Ethical journalism is the foundation of credibility. Journalists should adhere to established ethical guidelines and codes of conduct, such as those outlined by professional organizations like the Society of Professional Journalists (SPJ) or the Online News Association (ONA). These guidelines emphasize principles such as accuracy, fairness, objectivity, and transparency.

2. Verify Sources and Information

In the rush to break news, it's essential to prioritize accuracy over speed. Journalists should rigorously verify sources and information before publishing. Multiple credible sources should corroborate critical facts, and any uncertainty should be acknowledged transparently. Fact-checking and confirming information are crucial steps in the reporting process.

3. Transparency in Reporting

Transparency builds trust. Journalists should provide readers with insight into how stories are researched, reported, and edited. This includes disclosing potential conflicts of interest, sources' affiliations, and any known biases. When corrections are necessary, they should be issued promptly and prominently.

4. Avoid Sensationalism and Clickbait

Sensationalism and clickbait headlines may attract attention but erode trust in the long run. Journalists should prioritize accurate and informative headlines that reflect the content of the story. Avoiding sensationalism and maintaining a sober tone in reporting contributes to credibility.

5. Engage with the Audience

Building a relationship with the audience fosters trust. Journalists should actively engage with readers through comments, social media, and online discussions. Responding to reader questions, providing context, and acknowledging feedback demonstrate a commitment to transparency and accountability.

6. Diversify Sources and Perspectives

Balance and diversity in sourcing are essential. Journalists should seek out a range of perspectives and voices to provide a comprehensive view of a story. Avoiding reliance on a single source or a narrow range of viewpoints enhances credibility and reduces the risk of bias.

7. Fact-Based Reporting

Emphasize fact-based reporting over conjecture or opinion. Clearly distinguish between news reporting and opinion pieces. Ensure that the facts are the foundation of news stories, and if analysis or commentary is included, make it explicit.

8. Responsible Handling of Sensitive Topics

When reporting on sensitive topics such as trauma, tragedy, or personal crises, exercise sensitivity and discretion. Consider the potential impact of reporting on affected individuals and communities. Seek consent when appropriate, and minimize harm through responsible reporting.

9. Data Ethics

In data-driven journalism, ethical considerations are paramount. Journalists should handle data responsibly, ensuring privacy and security. Data should be obtained legally and ethically, and any analysis or presentation of data should be accurate and unbiased.

10. Media Literacy and Education

Promote media literacy and educate the audience. Journalists can contribute to media literacy efforts by explaining how news is produced, offering tips for critical evaluation of sources, and debunking common misinformation. Informed readers are more likely to trust credible sources.

11. Uphold Independence

Journalistic independence is a bedrock principle. Reporters should resist undue influence or pressure from external sources, whether they are advertisers, sponsors, or political entities. Independence ensures that reporting serves the public interest rather than specific agendas.

12. Learn and Adapt

The digital landscape is constantly evolving. Journalists should stay informed about emerging technologies, digital trends, and changes in audience behavior. Continuous learning and adaptation are essential for remaining relevant and credible in online journalism.

By consistently applying these strategies and principles, internet journalists can uphold their credibility and maintain the trust of their readers. Trust is hard-earned but easily lost, and safeguarding it is essential for the long-term success and impact of internet journalism.

In the subsequent chapters, we will delve deeper into specific ethical considerations and practical guidelines that can help journalists navigate the complexities of online reporting while upholding their commitment to truth, accuracy, and integrity.

Fact-checking and Verification

In the digital age, where information can spread rapidly and misinformation is prevalent, fact-checking and verification are paramount for maintaining the credibility of internet journalism. Journalists must adhere to rigorous fact-checking standards to ensure the accuracy and reliability of their reporting. Here are key principles and practices for effective fact-checking and verification:

1. Source Reliability

Verifying the reliability of sources is the first step in fact-checking. Journalists should evaluate the credibility of individuals, organizations, and institutions providing information. Established and reputable sources are more likely to provide accurate and trustworthy information.

2. Cross-Checking with Multiple Sources

Corroborating information with multiple independent sources is a fundamental practice. Relying on a single source, especially an unverified one, can lead to inaccuracies. Journalists should cross-check facts and claims with a variety of reputable sources to ensure accuracy.

3. Documenting Sources

Thorough documentation of sources is essential. Journalists should keep detailed records of interviews, documents, and data sources. This documentation not only aids in verification but also serves as a reference for future reporting and potential legal issues.

4. Evaluating Primary vs. Secondary Sources

Distinguishing between primary and secondary sources is crucial. Primary sources provide firsthand information, while secondary sources may rely on others' reporting. Journalists should prioritize primary sources when available and attribute information accurately.

5. Fact-checking Organizations

Utilize fact-checking organizations and databases. Many reputable organizations specialize in fact-checking claims and statements. Collaborating with these organizations or referencing their findings can enhance the accuracy of reporting.

6. Verifying Visual Content

Visual content, including images and videos, should undergo rigorous verification. Journalists should examine metadata, reverse image search, and consult experts when necessary to confirm the authenticity and context of visual material.

7. Confirming Dates and Timelines

Timeliness and sequencing of events are essential in news reporting. Journalists should confirm dates and timelines meticulously, avoiding inaccuracies that can arise from misunderstandings or misinterpretations of temporal details.

8. Addressing Misinformation

Journalists have a responsibility to correct and counteract misinformation. When errors are identified, they should be corrected promptly, prominently, and transparently. Additionally, providing context and fact-based analysis can help combat misinformation effectively.

9. Legal and Ethical Considerations

Fact-checking should align with legal and ethical standards. Journalists must respect privacy, avoid defamation, and handle sensitive information responsibly while fact-checking. Ethical considerations should guide the process.

10. Accountability

Accountability is a key aspect of fact-checking. Journalists should be accountable for their reporting and decisions. If errors occur, they should take responsibility, issue corrections, and learn from the experience to prevent future inaccuracies.

11. Ongoing Training and Resources

Journalists should stay updated on fact-checking techniques and best practices. Training programs, workshops, and resources offered by professional organizations can help improve fact-checking skills. Staying informed about emerging digital tools and technologies for fact-checking is also essential.

12. Collaborative Fact-checking

Collaboration with other news organizations and fact-checkers can enhance the accuracy and impact of fact-checking efforts. Sharing resources, expertise, and findings can help expose misinformation and uphold journalistic standards collectively.

By adhering to these fact-checking and verification principles, internet journalists can bolster the accuracy and reliability of their reporting. Fact-checking not only serves as a safeguard against misinformation but also demonstrates a commitment to journalistic integrity and accountability. In the digital age, where information is both abundant and vulnerable to distortion, fact-checking remains a cornerstone of credible journalism.

Chapter 4: Writing for the Web

Adapting Writing Styles for Online Readers

In the digital realm, the way content is written can significantly impact its reception and engagement with online readers. Internet journalism requires a unique approach to writing that caters to the preferences and behaviors of the online audience. Here, we explore key considerations for adapting writing styles to effectively reach and resonate with online readers:

1. Clarity and Conciseness

Online readers often skim content rather than reading it word-for-word. To capture their attention and convey information effectively, journalists should prioritize clarity and conciseness. Use clear and straightforward language, avoid jargon, and get to the point quickly. Break content into easily digestible chunks with subheadings and bullet points.

2. Scannability and Visual Appeal

Web readers appreciate content that is easy to scan. Use descriptive subheadings that provide an overview of the content. Incorporate visuals such as images, infographics, and videos to complement text and break up long blocks of content. Visual elements enhance the overall reading experience and help convey information more efficiently.

3. Use of Hyperlinks

Hyperlinks are a fundamental feature of web content. Use them strategically to provide additional context, sources, or related articles. Ensure that hyperlink text is descriptive and indicates where the link will take the reader. Avoid overloading content with too many hyperlinks, which can be distracting.

4. Mobile-Friendly Writing

With a significant portion of online readers accessing content on mobile devices, it's crucial to write content that is mobile-friendly. Short paragraphs, concise sentences, and responsive design ensure that content is easily readable on smaller screens. Test content on various devices to optimize the mobile reading experience.

5. Engaging Headlines and Leads

Compelling headlines and engaging leads are essential for capturing the reader's interest. Craft headlines that are informative, attention-grabbing, and indicative of the article's content. The lead, or introductory paragraph, should provide a concise summary of the article's main points, encouraging readers to continue.

6. Conversational Tone

Online readers often prefer a conversational tone. Write in a way that feels approachable and relatable, as if you're having a conversation with the reader. Avoid overly formal or academic language that can create barriers to understanding.

7. Use of Lists and Bulleted Points

Lists and bulleted points are effective for presenting information in a structured and digestible format. When discussing multiple key points, consider presenting them as lists, which are visually appealing and aid in retention.

8. Engage with Multimedia

Incorporate multimedia elements like images, videos, and interactive graphics to enhance storytelling. Visual and interactive elements can provide additional context and engagement, making the content more appealing to online readers.

9. Audience-Centric Approach

Consider the needs and interests of your target audience when writing. What questions might they have? What information would be most valuable to them? Tailor your content to address their concerns and preferences.

10. Regular Updates

Online readers appreciate fresh content. Regularly update articles, especially if they involve rapidly evolving topics. Indicate the date of the last update to signal to readers that the information is current.

11. SEO Best Practices

Optimize content for search engines by incorporating relevant keywords naturally. However, avoid keyword stuffing, which can detract from the readability and quality of the content. Aim for a balance between SEO optimization and user-friendly writing.

12. Proofreading and Editing

Errors and typos can undermine the credibility of online content. Thoroughly proofread and edit articles before publication. Consider enlisting the help of editors or using proofreading tools to catch mistakes.

Adapting writing styles for online readers requires a blend of clear communication, visual appeal, and engagement strategies. By implementing these considerations, internet journalists can create content that resonates with their online audience, fosters reader engagement, and maintains the credibility of their publications.

In the following chapters, we will explore practical techniques and case studies that demonstrate the effective application of these writing principles in internet journalism.

SEO and Its Role in Online Journalism

Search Engine Optimization (SEO) is a fundamental aspect of internet journalism that influences how content is discovered and ranked by search engines like

Google, Bing, and Yahoo. SEO plays a crucial role in driving organic traffic to news websites and increasing the visibility of news stories. Understanding the principles of SEO is essential for internet journalists. Here, we delve into the significance of SEO and how it impacts online journalism:

1. Enhancing Discoverability

One of the primary roles of SEO is to enhance the discoverability of news content. When readers search for information using search engines, they rely on specific keywords and phrases. Effective SEO practices ensure that news articles are optimized with relevant keywords, making them more likely to appear in search results. This increases the chances of reaching a broader audience.

2. Attracting Targeted Audiences

SEO allows news organizations to attract targeted audiences interested in specific topics. By aligning content with popular search queries related to breaking news, trending stories, or niche subjects, journalists can connect with readers actively seeking information in those areas. This targeted approach increases the relevance of the content to the audience.

3. Competing in a Crowded Digital Space

The digital space is crowded with news websites and content creators. SEO provides a competitive edge by ensuring that a news story ranks well in search engine results pages (SERPs). Articles appearing at the top of

SERPs are more likely to be clicked by users, giving news organizations a competitive advantage in capturing reader attention.

4. Boosting Credibility and Trust

High search engine rankings can boost the credibility and trustworthiness of news sources. Readers often perceive articles that appear on the first page of search results as more authoritative and reliable. A strong SEO strategy can help establish a news organization as a trusted source of information.

5. Adapting to Changing Trends

SEO is not static; it evolves with changing search engine algorithms and user behaviors. Internet journalists must stay informed about SEO trends and updates to maintain the visibility of their content. This adaptability ensures that news articles remain relevant and competitive in the digital landscape.

6. Leveraging Multimedia Content

SEO is not limited to written content. Multimedia elements, including images, videos, and infographics, can also be optimized for search. Journalists should use descriptive file names, alt tags, and captions to make multimedia content more discoverable and accessible.

7. Balancing SEO and Quality Journalism

Maintaining a balance between SEO optimization and quality journalism is critical. While SEO is essential for discoverability, content should never prioritize keywords over accuracy, integrity, and ethical reporting. Ethical and responsible journalism should always be the primary focus.

8. Analytics and Measurement

SEO efforts should be measured and analyzed to assess their effectiveness. News organizations can use web analytics tools to track the performance of their content, monitor keyword rankings, and gain insights into audience behavior. This data informs editorial decisions and helps refine SEO strategies.

9. User Experience and Mobile Optimization

Search engines consider user experience when ranking content. News websites that are mobile-friendly, load quickly, and provide a seamless reading experience are more likely to rank higher. Journalists should ensure that their content is optimized for mobile devices to cater to the growing mobile audience.

10. Ethical Considerations

Ethical considerations are paramount in SEO. Journalists should avoid manipulative tactics such as keyword stuffing or link schemes that violate search engine guidelines. Ethical SEO practices align with the principles of responsible journalism.

In summary, SEO is a dynamic and essential component of online journalism. By understanding and implementing SEO best practices, journalists can improve the discoverability of their content, connect with targeted audiences, and enhance the credibility of their news organizations. SEO is a tool that empowers internet journalists to navigate the digital landscape and reach readers in an increasingly competitive online environment.

Crafting Engaging Headlines and Subheadings

In the fast-paced world of internet journalism, headlines and subheadings play a pivotal role in capturing readers' attention, providing context, and guiding them through the content. Crafting compelling headlines and subheadings is both an art and a science, as they must be optimized for search engines (SEO) while also engaging human readers. Here are key strategies and considerations for creating headlines and subheadings that resonate with online audiences:

1. Clarity and Conciseness

Headlines should convey the main point of the article clearly and concisely. Avoid vague or ambiguous language that may leave readers unsure of what to expect. Use straightforward and descriptive wording that provides a glimpse of the article's content.

2. Keyword Integration

Incorporate relevant keywords naturally into headlines and subheadings. This not only improves SEO but also ensures that the content aligns with the reader's search intent. However, avoid keyword stuffing, which can make headlines appear spammy and less engaging.

3. Attention-Grabbing Hooks

Engaging headlines often include attention-grabbing hooks. Pose questions, use strong action verbs, or create a sense of urgency to pique readers' curiosity. A well-crafted hook encourages readers to delve further into the article.

4. Accuracy and Honesty

Headlines should accurately reflect the content of the article. Misleading or clickbait-style headlines can erode trust with readers and result in high bounce rates (readers quickly leaving the page). Honesty and transparency in headlines are essential.

5. Subheadings as Signposts

Subheadings serve as signposts that guide readers through the article's structure. Use subheadings to break content into logical sections and summarize key points. This enhances readability and helps readers quickly find the information they seek.

6. Visual Appeal

The visual presentation of headlines and subheadings matters. Choose fonts, styles, and formatting that are visually appealing and consistent with the overall design of the website. Ensure that headlines stand out and are easy to distinguish from the body text.

7. Audience-Centric Language

Consider the language and terminology that resonates with your target audience. Tailor headlines and subheadings to the preferences and interests of your readers. This audience-centric approach increases engagement.

8. A/B Testing

A/B testing involves experimenting with different headline variations to determine which ones perform best with your audience. It can help refine headline strategies and identify which types of headlines generate higher click-through rates.

9. Length Matters

Pay attention to headline length. While there is no strict character limit, shorter headlines are often more effective because they are easier to scan and understand quickly. However, longer headlines can be appropriate for in-depth or feature articles.

10. Mobile Optimization

Consider the mobile reading experience when crafting headlines and subheadings. Ensure that they are concise and visually appealing on smaller screens. Mobile optimization is crucial, as many readers access content on smartphones and tablets.

11. Consistency and Branding

Maintain consistency in your headline style and branding. A recognizable and consistent format helps readers identify your content and builds trust over time. This includes using a consistent tone, style, and voice.

12. Testing and Iteration

Effective headline writing is an iterative process. Continuously analyze the performance of your headlines and subheadings. Monitor metrics such as click-through rates, time spent on page, and bounce rates to refine your approach.

Engaging headlines and subheadings are gateways to your content, enticing readers to explore further. They are vital tools for capturing attention, conveying the essence of your articles, and enhancing the overall reader experience. By mastering the art of crafting compelling headlines and subheadings, internet journalists can improve the discoverability and engagement of their content in the digital landscape.

Chapter 5: Multimedia Journalism

Incorporating Images, Videos, and Infographics

Multimedia elements such as images, videos, and infographics are powerful tools in the arsenal of internet journalism. They not only enhance storytelling but also cater to the diverse preferences of online audiences. Incorporating multimedia elements effectively can elevate the impact and engagement of news articles. Here's a closer look at how to harness the potential of these multimedia components:

1. Visual Storytelling

Visual storytelling is at the heart of multimedia journalism. Images and videos can convey information, evoke emotions, and provide context in a way that text alone cannot. Use visuals to complement and enrich the narrative of your news articles.

2. Diverse Media Formats

Offer a variety of media formats to cater to different audiences. Some readers prefer watching videos, while others may prefer viewing infographics or scrolling through image galleries. Providing options ensures that your content appeals to a broader range of users.

3. Contextual Relevance

Ensure that multimedia elements are contextually relevant to the story. Each image, video clip, or infographic should contribute to the understanding of the article's topic. Avoid using visuals for purely decorative purposes.

4. Original Content

Whenever possible, create original multimedia content that supports your reporting. Original photographs, videos, and infographics add authenticity and value to your articles. Invest in high-quality equipment and editing tools to produce professional visuals.

5. Credible Sources

If you use visuals from external sources, ensure that they come from credible and reliable sources. Properly attribute and credit the source of the visuals. Respect copyright and licensing agreements when using third-party media.

6. Accessibility

Make your multimedia content accessible to all readers, including those with disabilities. Provide alternative text descriptions for images and captions for videos. Ensure that your media is compatible with screen readers and other assistive technologies.

7. Interactive Features

Consider incorporating interactive elements into your multimedia content. Interactive maps, timelines, and graphics can engage readers and allow them to explore the story in a more dynamic way. These features are especially effective for in-depth reporting.

8. Mobile Optimization

Optimize multimedia content for mobile devices, as a significant portion of online users access content on smartphones and tablets. Ensure that videos are responsive and that images load quickly on mobile connections.

9. Engaging Thumbnails and Previews

The first impression matters. Choose engaging thumbnails for videos and eye-catching preview images for articles with multimedia content. These visual cues entice users to click and engage with the content.

10. Collaborative Reporting

Collaborate with multimedia specialists and photographers to produce high-quality visuals. A team approach can lead to more compelling and impactful multimedia journalism.

11. Ethical Considerations

Apply ethical standards when selecting, editing, and presenting multimedia content. Respect the privacy and dignity of individuals depicted in images and videos. Ensure that visuals accurately represent the story and context.

12. Analyze Engagement Metrics

Monitor engagement metrics to understand how readers interact with multimedia content. Analyze data on video views, image clicks, and infographic interactions. Use this information to refine your multimedia strategy.

13. Storytelling Impact

Evaluate the impact of multimedia elements on your storytelling. Do visuals enhance understanding? Do they evoke emotions? Assess whether multimedia components contribute to the overall narrative and reader engagement.

Incorporating images, videos, and infographics is not merely an option in internet journalism; it's a necessity. These multimedia elements have the potential to make complex topics more accessible, engage readers on a deeper level, and enhance the overall quality of journalism in the digital age.

In the upcoming chapters, we will explore practical techniques, case studies, and best practices for effectively integrating multimedia elements into internet journalism.

Podcasting and Audio Journalism

Podcasting has emerged as a dynamic and engaging medium in the field of internet journalism. It offers a unique way to connect with audiences, convey information, and tell compelling stories through audio. Audio journalism, in the form of podcasts, has grown in popularity due to its accessibility and the ability to reach listeners on the go. Here's a closer look at how podcasting and audio journalism contribute to the multimedia landscape:

1. The Power of the Human Voice
Audio journalism harnesses the power of the human voice to communicate news, insights, and stories. Hearing voices, inflections, and emotions can create a more personal and immersive experience for listeners.

2. Storytelling in Audio Format
Podcasts excel at storytelling. They allow for in-depth exploration of topics, personal narratives, and interviews that captivate and inform listeners. The conversational tone of podcasts can draw audiences into the narrative.

3. Diverse Content Formats
Podcasting offers a diverse range of content formats, including news briefings, investigative reports, interview shows, documentaries, and more. This versatility allows journalists to tailor their content to different audiences and storytelling needs.

4. Accessibility and Convenience
Podcasts are highly accessible and convenient. Listeners can tune in from anywhere, whether during a commute, workout, or household chores. This flexibility enables news organizations to reach audiences in various settings.

5. Building a Loyal Audience

Podcasts can foster a sense of community and loyalty among listeners. Regular episodes and recurring segments create a connection with the audience, turning them into dedicated followers.

6. Engaging Interviews

Interview-style podcasts can feature prominent experts, public figures, or individuals with unique perspectives. Engaging interviews add depth and credibility to the journalism, providing valuable insights to the audience.

7. Investigative Journalism

Podcasts are an ideal platform for investigative journalism. They allow for in-depth examinations of complex issues, detailed storytelling, and the presentation of evidence, making them suitable for long-form investigative reporting.

8. Production Quality

High production quality is essential for audio journalism. Invest in quality recording equipment, sound editing software, and sound engineering to ensure clear and professional-sounding podcasts.

9. Storyboard and Scripting

Effective podcasting often involves storyboarding and scripting to organize content and ensure a cohesive narrative. While podcasts can have a spontaneous feel, having a structured plan enhances the storytelling.

10. Distribution and Promotion

Promoting podcasts is crucial for building an audience. Share episodes on your news website, social media, and podcast directories. Consider cross-promotions with other podcasts and collaborations with influencers.

11. Analytics and Feedback

Use analytics to track the performance of your podcasts. Monitor metrics like downloads, listens, and listener demographics to understand your audience better. Encourage feedback from listeners to improve content.

12. Ethical Considerations

Maintain ethical standards in audio journalism, just as in other forms of journalism. Ensure accuracy, fairness, and transparency in reporting. Respect privacy and obtain consent when recording individuals.

13. Accessibility Features

Make podcasts accessible to individuals with disabilities by providing transcripts or captions. Ensure that your podcast hosting platform allows for easy integration with accessibility tools.

14. Monetization Strategies

Consider monetization strategies such as sponsorships, advertising, or subscription models. Monetizing podcasts can support the sustainability of your journalism efforts.

15. Continuous Improvement

Podcasting is a dynamic field. Keep learning and improving your podcasting skills. Stay updated on industry trends, evolving technologies, and audience preferences.

Podcasting and audio journalism offer a rich and engaging way to connect with audiences, tell compelling stories, and disseminate news and information. As an integral part of multimedia journalism, podcasts contribute to the diverse landscape of internet journalism, providing a valuable platform for in-depth reporting and audience engagement.

In the upcoming chapters, we will explore practical techniques, case studies, and best practices for successfully producing and promoting podcasts as part of internet journalism.

Interactive Storytelling Techniques

Interactive storytelling is a dynamic and engaging approach that empowers readers to actively participate in the news narrative. It goes beyond traditional linear storytelling and allows readers to explore, interact, and make choices within a news story. Internet journalism can harness interactive storytelling techniques to create immersive and memorable experiences. Here's an in-depth look at how to effectively employ interactive storytelling:

1. Choose the Right Platform

Select the appropriate platform or tool for your interactive story. Various content management systems, plugins, and software offer interactive features. Consider your target audience and the technical capabilities of the chosen platform.

2. Storyboarding and Planning

Interactive stories require careful planning. Create a storyboard or flowchart to outline the narrative structure, decision points, and interactive elements. Consider how readers will navigate and engage with the content.

3. Engaging Visuals and Multimedia

Incorporate visuals, videos, infographics, and animations to enhance interactivity. Visuals should not only be eye-catching but also provide context and information. Multimedia elements can deepen the reader's understanding of the story.

4. Meaningful Choices

Offer readers meaningful choices that influence the direction of the narrative. Choices should be relevant to the story and have consequences that impact the outcome. This empowers readers and makes them active participants.

5. Multiple Story Paths

Interactive storytelling often involves multiple story paths or branching narratives. Depending on the choices readers make, they should experience different aspects of the story. Each path should contribute to the overall understanding.

6. Feedback and Consequences

Provide feedback to readers based on their choices. Explain the consequences of their actions and how they impact the story. This feedback adds depth to the interactive experience.

7. User-Friendly Design

Ensure that the interactive story has an intuitive and user-friendly design. Navigation should be seamless, and readers should easily understand how to interact with the content. Test the user experience extensively.

8. Accessibility

Make interactive stories accessible to all readers, including those with disabilities. Ensure compatibility with screen readers, provide alternative text for visuals, and consider color contrast for readability.

9. Mobile Optimization

Optimize interactive stories for mobile devices. Many readers access content on smartphones and tablets, so it's crucial that the interactive elements work smoothly on smaller screens.

10. Performance and Loading Times

Interactive features should load quickly and perform well. Slow loading times can frustrate readers and lead to high bounce rates. Optimize media files and interactive components for speed.

11. Collaborative Development

Collaborate with multimedia specialists, designers, and developers to create interactive stories. Effective interactive storytelling often involves a multidisciplinary team with expertise in different areas.

12. Engagement Analytics

Use analytics tools to track reader engagement with interactive stories. Monitor which choices readers make, how they navigate the story, and where they drop off. This data can inform future interactive storytelling efforts.

13. Ethical Considerations

Interactive storytelling should adhere to the same ethical standards as traditional journalism. Accuracy, fairness, and transparency are paramount. Ensure that the interactive elements do not compromise the integrity of the reporting.

14. Iteration and Feedback

Seek feedback from readers and colleagues to improve interactive storytelling. Continuously iterate on your techniques and approaches to enhance the user experience.

Interactive storytelling is a powerful way to captivate readers and immerse them in news narratives. It encourages active engagement, exploration, and a deeper understanding of complex issues. By employing these techniques effectively, internet journalists can create memorable and impactful interactive stories that resonate with their audience.

Chapter 6: Social Media and Journalism

Utilizing Social Platforms for News Dissemination

Social media has revolutionized the way news is disseminated, consumed, and engaged with. Internet journalism now thrives on various social platforms, leveraging their reach, immediacy, and interactivity to connect with a global audience. This chapter explores the integral role of social media in modern journalism and provides insights into effectively utilizing social platforms for news dissemination.

The Social Media Landscape

The digital age has witnessed the emergence of a diverse social media landscape, comprising platforms such as Facebook, Twitter, Instagram, LinkedIn, TikTok, YouTube, and more. Each platform offers unique opportunities and challenges for news organizations seeking to share their stories.

The Power of Real-Time Updates

Social media excels in delivering real-time updates and breaking news to audiences. News organizations can instantly share updates, eyewitness accounts, and live coverage, ensuring that readers stay informed as events unfold.

Audience Engagement and Interaction

Engagement is at the heart of social media. News organizations can engage with their audience through comments, likes, shares, and direct messages. This direct interaction fosters community building and enables immediate feedback.

Viral Potential and Amplification

The viral nature of social media can amplify news stories. A single share from a reputable source can lead to widespread dissemination, increasing the reach and impact of journalism.

Multimedia Storytelling

Social platforms facilitate multimedia storytelling. News organizations can leverage visuals, videos, infographics, and live streaming to convey information effectively and engage audiences.

Challenges and Ethical Considerations

While social media offers immense potential, it also presents challenges. Misinformation, ethical dilemmas, and privacy concerns are ever-present. Journalists must navigate these issues responsibly.

Social Media Strategy

Developing a comprehensive social media strategy is essential. It involves platform selection, content planning, engagement tactics, and crisis management to ensure that social media efforts align with journalistic integrity.

Measuring Impact

Analytics tools provide insights into the impact of social media efforts. Metrics such as engagement rates, reach, and referral traffic help news organizations assess the effectiveness of their social media campaigns.

Case Studies and Best Practices

Throughout this chapter, we'll delve into real-world case studies and best practices that highlight successful approaches to using social media in journalism. These examples showcase innovative strategies and the power of social platforms in news dissemination.

Social media has transformed journalism from a one-way communication model to a dynamic, interactive, and community-driven endeavor. By mastering the art of utilizing social platforms effectively, internet journalists can harness the full potential of these platforms to reach, engage, and inform a global audience.

In the subsequent sections, we will explore each aspect of social media's impact on journalism in greater detail, offering practical insights and actionable strategies for internet journalists.

Managing Online Communities and Engagement

In the ever-evolving landscape of social media and journalism, managing online communities and fostering engagement is a pivotal aspect of internet journalism. This section explores the strategies and considerations involved in effectively overseeing and nurturing online communities on various social media platforms. It also delves into the methods for engaging with audiences, building a sense of community, and fostering meaningful interactions.

The Role of Online Communities

Online communities serve as the backbone of social media-driven journalism. They provide a platform for readers, viewers, and listeners to connect, share their perspectives, and engage with news content. Understanding the significance of these communities is essential for internet journalists seeking to harness the power of social media for news dissemination.

Community Building Strategies

Building and maintaining online communities require deliberate strategies. Internet journalists should create spaces where users feel welcome, respected, and valued. This involves setting community guidelines, moderating discussions, and addressing issues promptly.

Audience Engagement Techniques

Engaging with the audience is a dynamic process. Journalists can use techniques such as responding to comments, hosting Q&A sessions, conducting polls, and encouraging user-generated content to foster engagement. Authenticity and responsiveness are key to building trust and rapport.

Content Curation and Sharing

The content shared within online communities should align with the interests and needs of the audience. Curating and sharing relevant news stories, updates, and multimedia content ensures that the community remains informed and engaged.

Moderation and Conflict Resolution

Effective community management includes moderation to maintain a respectful and constructive environment. Addressing conflicts and disruptive behavior promptly is crucial to preserving the integrity of the community.

Data and Analytics Insights

Utilizing data and analytics tools can provide valuable insights into community behavior and preferences. Journalists can analyze engagement metrics, sentiment analysis, and demographic data to tailor content and engagement strategies.

Ethical Considerations

Ethical standards should be upheld in all community interactions. Respecting user privacy, avoiding bias, and adhering to journalistic principles are essential to maintaining credibility and trust within online communities.

Crisis Management

Being prepared for crises is vital. News organizations should have crisis management protocols in place to address sensitive issues or controversies that may arise within their online communities.

Fostering Inclusivity and Diversity

Online communities should reflect diversity and inclusivity. Journalists should actively seek out diverse voices and perspectives, ensuring that the community represents a wide range of viewpoints.

Measuring Community Impact

Measuring the impact of online communities involves assessing metrics such as engagement rates, user growth, and the quality of discussions. These insights help news organizations gauge the effectiveness of their community management efforts.

Managing online communities and fostering engagement within the realm of social media and journalism is both an art and a science. It requires a deep understanding of audience behavior, a commitment to ethical practices, and a dedication to creating spaces where meaningful interactions can flourish. In doing so, internet journalists can harness the collective power of their communities to enhance news dissemination and build lasting connections with their audience.

Dealing with Fake News and Misinformation

In today's digital landscape, where social media platforms serve as significant sources of news dissemination, the issue of fake news and misinformation has taken center stage. This subsection within Chapter 6 explores the complexities of managing the spread of false information and maintaining the credibility of internet journalism.

The Rise of Fake News

The internet has provided an unprecedented platform for the rapid dissemination of information. Unfortunately, this has also given rise to the spread of fake news, which can encompass fabricated stories, misleading headlines, and manipulated visuals.

The internet has ushered in an era of unparalleled connectivity and information sharing, transforming the way news is disseminated and consumed. However, this digital revolution has also given rise to a significant challenge—fake news. Fake news encompasses a wide range of deceptive content, including fabricated stories, misleading headlines, and manipulated visuals. Understanding the scope and impact of this issue is paramount for journalists operating in the digital sphere.

The Digital Information Explosion

The internet has democratized information dissemination, allowing individuals from all corners of the globe to publish and share content. This explosion of digital information has revolutionized journalism, providing opportunities for citizen journalists, bloggers, and independent news outlets to contribute to the global news landscape. However, this democratization has a double-edged sword.

The Proliferation of Falsehoods

With the ease of publishing and sharing on the internet comes the risk of misinformation. False information, whether created for malicious intent or due to a lack of verification, can spread rapidly across social media platforms, websites, and messaging apps. This proliferation of falsehoods has the potential to distort public perception, influence elections, and even incite real-world harm.

Misleading Headlines and Manipulated Visuals

Fake news takes various forms, including misleading headlines designed to grab attention and manipulate emotions. Such headlines often play on readers' curiosity or outrage, enticing them to click and share without critically evaluating the content. Additionally, fake news frequently incorporates manipulated visuals, such as photos and videos altered to convey false narratives.

Impact on Journalism Credibility

For journalists operating in the digital age, the prevalence of fake news poses a significant threat to their credibility. Audiences may become skeptical of news sources, and trust in journalism as a whole can be eroded. In this environment, responsible reporting and the commitment to truth become more critical than ever.

Countering Fake News Challenges

Countering fake news challenges journalists to adapt their practices. Fact-checking and source verification become essential tools for separating fact from fiction. Journalists must also be vigilant in avoiding the unintentional amplification of false information while ensuring that corrections are promptly issued when errors occur.

The Responsibility of Media Literacy

Media literacy plays a pivotal role in addressing the spread of fake news. Educating the public on how to critically assess information sources, recognize biases, and employ fact-checking techniques is a proactive approach to mitigating the impact of misinformation.

Collaboration and Ethical Reporting

Journalists are not alone in the battle against fake news. Collaboration with fact-checking organizations, fellow journalists, and social media platforms can enhance efforts to verify information and prevent the dissemination of false news. Ethical reporting practices, including transparent sourcing and corrections, remain fundamental in preserving the integrity of journalism in the digital age.

Conclusion

The rise of fake news in the digital era is a complex and multifaceted challenge. It underscores the need for vigilance, responsible reporting, and media literacy. By understanding the nature and impact of fake news, journalists can better equip themselves to navigate this evolving landscape and fulfill their essential role as purveyors of accurate and trustworthy information.

In the subsequent sections of this chapter, we will explore practical strategies, best practices, and real-world case studies that shed further light on addressing the issue of fake news and maintaining the credibility of internet journalism.

Identifying Misinformation

Identifying misinformation is the crucial first step in combatting fake news. In an era where false information can quickly go viral, journalists must possess the skills and strategies to recognize false or misleading content. This section explores the techniques and practices that journalists can employ to discern fact from fiction, ensuring the accuracy and credibility of news content.

Source Verification

One of the fundamental techniques for identifying misinformation is source verification. Journalists must meticulously assess the credibility of the sources they rely on for information. This involves confirming the identity and expertise of the source, checking for any potential biases, and evaluating the source's track record for accuracy.

Example: Imagine a breaking news story emerges on social media, claiming that a prominent scientist has made a groundbreaking discovery in a specific field. Journalists, before reporting on this, should verify the source of this information. They might investigate whether the source is a reputable scientific institution or a trusted news outlet. If the source is an obscure blog or an unverified social media account, it raises red flags about the credibility of the information.

Cross-Referencing

Cross-referencing is a powerful tool for fact-checking and identifying misinformation. Journalists should cross-reference information from multiple sources to confirm its accuracy. If a piece of news is reported by several reputable news organizations, it is more likely to be accurate. Conversely, if it's only found on a single, unverified source, it may warrant skepticism.

Example: Suppose there's a news report circulating about a natural disaster in a remote region. To confirm the accuracy of this report, journalists can cross-reference information with government agencies, local authorities, and established news outlets. Consistency in the reporting from multiple credible sources provides greater confidence in the accuracy of the news.

Fact-Checking

Fact-checking is a dedicated practice employed by journalists to scrutinize claims, statements, and data presented in news stories. Fact-checkers use various tools and methodologies to assess the accuracy of information. This can involve investigating claims, consulting experts, and reviewing primary sources.

Example: During an election campaign, a candidate makes a claim about a specific policy's impact on the economy. Fact-checkers would research economic data, consult economists and experts, and assess the candidate's statement against credible sources to determine its accuracy. Fact-checking organizations often publish detailed reports explaining their findings, providing transparency to readers.

Digital Forensics

In the digital age, misinformation can be disseminated through manipulated visuals and videos. Digital forensics techniques involve analyzing images and videos to detect signs of manipulation or editing. This practice can reveal the authenticity of multimedia content.

Example: A viral image claims to depict a recent protest event. Journalists can employ digital forensics tools to examine metadata, perform reverse image searches, and analyze the image for signs of manipulation, such as inconsistent lighting or cloned objects. Such analysis can help determine whether the image accurately represents the reported event.

Social Media Scrutiny

Misinformation often spreads rapidly on social media platforms. Journalists should scrutinize information found on social media, considering factors such as the source's credibility, the number of shares and likes, and the presence of any fact-checking labels or warnings.

Example: A video circulating on social media purports to show a major political event. Journalists can examine the source of the video, check for any contextual information or labels provided by the platform, and assess whether the video has been independently verified by reputable news outlets.

By employing these techniques and practices, journalists can serve as gatekeepers of accurate information in an age of rampant misinformation. These methods not only help identify falsehoods but also contribute to maintaining the trust and credibility of journalism in the digital realm.

Fact-Checking and Verification

Fact-checking organizations have assumed a critical role in the ongoing battle against fake news and misinformation. These organizations play a pivotal role in verifying information, scrutinizing claims, and providing accurate assessments of the veracity of news stories. This section highlights the indispensable role of fact-checking organizations, their methodologies, and the significance of collaboration between journalists and fact-checkers to uphold the truth.

The Role of Fact-Checking Organizations

Fact-checking organizations are dedicated entities that specialize in assessing the accuracy of claims and statements made in news stories, political discourse, and public statements. They serve as independent arbiters of truth, providing impartial evaluations of the information presented to the public.

Example: During an election campaign, a political candidate makes a claim regarding a proposed policy's impact on healthcare costs. A fact-checking organization, operating independently from political parties and news outlets, takes on the task of investigating this claim. They scrutinize data, consult experts in healthcare economics, and assess the candidate's statement in the context of the available evidence. The fact-checking organization then publishes a report detailing the accuracy of the claim, presenting their findings to the public.

Fact-Checking Methodologies

Fact-checking organizations employ rigorous methodologies to assess the accuracy of claims and statements. These methodologies often involve thorough research, consultation with experts, and an examination of primary sources. Fact-checkers use a variety of tools and resources to verify information, including databases of factual information, archives of statements by public figures, and access to subject matter experts.

Example: A public figure makes a statement about climate change during a televised interview. A fact-checker will begin by researching the scientific consensus on climate change, consulting climate scientists and experts, and reviewing relevant scientific studies. They will also examine the historical record of statements made by the public figure on the topic. This comprehensive investigation forms the basis for the fact-checker's assessment of the statement's accuracy.

Collaboration with Journalists

Collaboration between journalists and fact-checkers is pivotal in ensuring the accuracy and credibility of news reporting. Journalists often work in tandem with fact-checking organizations to verify claims and statements made by public figures, politicians, or sources in news stories. This collaborative approach helps maintain journalistic integrity and upholds the commitment to truth.

Example: A breaking news story includes a statement from a government official regarding a public health crisis. The news organization covering the story collaborates with a fact-checking organization to verify the accuracy of the official's statement. Fact-checkers independently investigate the claim while journalists continue to report on the developing story. Once the fact-check is complete, the news organization can update its reporting with the verified information, ensuring the public receives accurate and trustworthy news.

Importance of Transparency

Fact-checking organizations prioritize transparency in their assessments. They provide clear explanations of their methodologies, sources, and the evidence supporting their conclusions. Transparency is essential for building trust with the public and allowing readers to understand the basis for fact-checking judgments.

Example: In a fact-check report, the organization not only declares a statement as "True" or "False" but also provides a detailed breakdown of their investigation. This includes references to scientific studies, interviews with experts, and an explanation of how they arrived at their verdict. Such transparency allows readers to evaluate the credibility of the fact-checking process.

Educating the Public

Fact-checking organizations also play a role in educating the public about critical thinking and media literacy. They often provide resources and guidelines for consumers of news to evaluate information critically, identify misinformation, and assess the reliability of sources.

Example: Fact-checking organizations may publish articles or guides on how to spot false information, recognize common tactics used in misleading claims, and conduct independent research to verify information before sharing it.

In summary, fact-checking organizations serve as invaluable allies in the battle against fake news and misinformation. Their methodologies, dedication to transparency, and collaborative efforts with journalists contribute to upholding the truth in journalism. By working together, journalists and fact-checkers can ensure that the public receives accurate and reliable information, even in the face of a barrage of false claims and misinformation.

This subsection highlights the essential role of fact-checking organizations in verifying information and upholding the accuracy of news reporting. The provided examples illustrate real-world scenarios where fact-checking organizations collaborate with journalists to assess the accuracy of claims and statements.

Ethical Reporting Amidst Misinformation

Maintaining ethical reporting standards is of utmost importance when dealing with misinformation. Internet journalists have a critical role in ensuring that they do not inadvertently contribute to the spread of false or unverified information. This section emphasizes the ethical responsibilities of journalists in an era where the accuracy of information is often compromised.

Avoiding Amplification of Unverified Information

One of the primary ethical considerations when confronted with misinformation is the avoidance of amplification. Journalists must exercise caution to prevent the inadvertent dissemination of false or misleading claims. Amplifying unverified information can contribute to its spread and further confuse the audience.

Example: A viral social media post claims that a popular food product causes a severe health condition. While the post gains traction, it lacks credible scientific evidence to support the claim. An internet journalist is approached by several readers who inquire about the post. Instead of simply repeating the unverified claim, the journalist takes an ethical approach by conducting independent research, consulting experts, and providing a well-informed response that outlines the lack of scientific evidence to substantiate the claim.

Prompt Corrections and Updates

In the fast-paced digital news environment, errors can occur. When journalists discover inaccuracies or errors in their reporting, it is their ethical obligation to promptly correct and update the information. Transparent corrections not only uphold journalistic integrity but also demonstrate a commitment to accuracy.

Example: A news article erroneously reports the date of a significant historical event. After the error is identified, the internet journalist issues a correction at the top of the article, clearly stating the accurate date and acknowledging the mistake. Additionally, the journalist adds an editor's note explaining the correction and the steps taken to rectify the error.

Responsible Sourcing and Attribution

Internet journalists must practice responsible sourcing and attribution when reporting on information that may be tainted by misinformation. They should be diligent in tracing the origins of claims and statements, giving appropriate credit to credible sources, and clearly labeling information that is unverified or comes from unreliable sources.

Example: A breaking news story emerges regarding a potential health crisis. The journalist reporting on the story attributes the information to the relevant health authorities, medical experts, and credible news outlets known for their accuracy. They also include a disclaimer indicating that the situation is rapidly evolving, and ongoing verification is in progress.

Avoiding Clickbait and Sensationalism

Sensationalizing or exaggerating the impact of misinformation for the sake of generating clicks or views is an unethical practice. Internet journalists should refrain from using clickbait headlines or hyperbolic language that may mislead the audience.

Example: A news outlet reports on a potential security breach affecting a popular software application. While the situation is concerning, the journalist avoids sensationalizing the issue in the headline or using alarmist language. Instead, they provide a factual and balanced account of the situation, including steps users can take to protect themselves.

Editorial Oversight and Accountability

Editorial oversight plays a crucial role in maintaining ethical reporting standards. News organizations should establish clear guidelines for fact-checking, corrections, and responsible reporting. Accountability mechanisms should be in place to address ethical lapses or inaccuracies promptly.

Example: A news organization has a dedicated editorial team responsible for reviewing and fact-checking all content before publication. If an error or ethical concern arises, the organization has a clear process for addressing the issue, issuing corrections, and, if necessary, holding individuals accountable.

Educating the Audience

Journalists can also contribute to ethical reporting by educating their audience about the challenges of misinformation and the importance of critical thinking. This can include articles or segments explaining how to evaluate sources, spot misinformation, and seek out verified information.

Example: A news outlet produces a series of articles and videos that provide tips and guidelines for their audience on how to critically assess information sources, verify claims, and differentiate between reliable and unreliable news outlets.

In summary, ethical reporting amidst misinformation is a foundational principle of internet journalism. Upholding ethical standards not only safeguards the credibility of journalism but also empowers the audience to navigate the complex landscape of information in the digital age.

Media Literacy and Public Education

Promoting media literacy among the audience is an effective strategy for addressing misinformation. Educating the public on how to critically evaluate news sources, distinguish between reliable and unreliable information, and identify potential red flags is a proactive approach to countering the spread of false news.

Platform Responsibility and Regulation

Social media and online platforms play a significant role in the dissemination of news. This section explores the responsibilities of these platforms in combatting fake news and the potential measures they can implement to mitigate the impact of misinformation. It also touches upon the evolving legal and regulatory landscape surrounding misinformation.

Case Studies and Best Practices

To provide practical insights, this subsection includes real-world case studies and best practices that illustrate successful approaches to identifying, addressing, and preventing fake news. These examples serve as valuable resources for internet journalists navigating the complex terrain of misinformation.

Dealing with fake news and misinformation is a critical aspect of social media-driven journalism. By addressing this issue within the context of "Chapter 6: Social Media and Journalism," this subsection aims to equip journalists with the knowledge and tools needed to confront falsehoods while preserving the credibility and integrity of digital journalism.

Chapter 7: Data Journalism and Visualization

Introduction to Data Journalism

In the digital age, data has assumed a central role in journalism. The volume and accessibility of data have transformed how journalists approach storytelling. It allows them to move beyond anecdotal evidence and uncover patterns, trends, and insights that traditional reporting methods may miss. Data can be sourced from various places, including government databases, public records, surveys, and even social media, providing a rich source of information for journalists.

Data-Driven Storytelling

Data journalism is about more than numbers; it's about telling meaningful stories with data. Journalists use data to investigate issues, answer questions, and reveal the hidden aspects of a story. Data-driven storytelling enhances the depth and impact of reporting. For example, data can be used to analyze crime rates in a city over time, track the spread of diseases, or understand the economic impact of a policy change. By translating data into narratives, journalists make complex topics accessible to a broader audience.

Data Journalism Ethics

Ethical considerations are paramount in data journalism. Journalists must navigate a range of ethical challenges, including privacy concerns, accuracy, and transparency. When working with data, it's crucial to ensure that data is collected and used responsibly. This includes obtaining consent when necessary, protecting the identities of individuals, and verifying the accuracy of data sources. Journalists must also be transparent about their methods, explaining how they collected, analyzed, and interpreted the data.

Data Visualization

Data visualization is a powerful tool in data journalism. It involves presenting data in a visual format, such as charts, graphs, maps, and interactive visuals. Effective data visualization enhances understanding and engagement with the information. Journalists use data visualization to simplify complex data, highlight key trends, and make data accessible to a broader audience. Visualization tools and techniques enable journalists to convey their findings more effectively. For instance, a journalist investigating climate change might use interactive maps to illustrate temperature trends over time, making the data more engaging and informative.

Data Journalism in Practice

Data journalism isn't confined to a single field or topic; it can be applied to virtually any subject. From political reporting and environmental investigations to healthcare analysis and economic trends, data journalism empowers journalists to explore diverse areas of interest. In practice, data journalists collect, clean, and analyze data to uncover compelling stories. They collaborate with experts, employ statistical techniques, and use visualization tools to present their findings. Data journalism has a broad impact, influencing public discourse, policy decisions, and public awareness.

In the following pages of this chapter, we will delve deeper into each of these aspects, providing practical guidance, examples, and case studies that illustrate the transformative potential of data journalism. We will explore data sources and tools, data visualization techniques, and the ethical considerations that guide data journalism practice. Whether you're an aspiring data journalist or a seasoned professional, this chapter aims to equip you with the knowledge and skills needed to harness the power of data for impactful storytelling.

Data Sources and Tools for Journalists

Diverse Data Sources

In the realm of data journalism, access to diverse and reliable data sources is fundamental. Journalists can obtain data from a wide range of places, each offering unique insights and opportunities for storytelling:

- **Government Databases:** Government agencies at local, regional, and national levels often maintain extensive databases on topics such as public spending, crime statistics, healthcare, and demographics. Access to these databases can be invaluable for investigative reporting and data-driven stories.

- **Public Records:** Public records contain a wealth of information on individuals, businesses, and organizations. These records, which include property records, court documents, and business registrations, can serve as valuable sources for in-depth reporting.

- **Surveys and Polls:** Surveys and polls conducted by reputable organizations provide data on public opinion, consumer behavior, and societal trends. Journalists can analyze survey results to uncover insights into various topics, from political preferences to lifestyle choices.

- **Social Media Data:** Social media platforms generate vast amounts of data every day. This data can offer insights into trends, public sentiment, and emerging issues. By tapping into social media data, journalists can gain a real-time understanding of public discourse.

- **Scientific Research:** Academic research and scientific studies provide data on a wide range of subjects, including health, climate, and social behavior. Journalists can collaborate with researchers or access published studies to inform their reporting.

Data Collection and Cleaning

Collecting and cleaning data is a critical step in data journalism. Journalists often encounter raw data that requires preparation before analysis. This process may involve:

- **Data Scraping:** Journalists can use web scraping tools to extract data from websites, turning unstructured information into usable datasets.

- **Data Cleaning:** Data may contain errors, inconsistencies, or missing values. Journalists must clean and preprocess the data to ensure accuracy and reliability.

- **Data Verification:** Verifying the authenticity and accuracy of data is essential. Journalists must confirm the credibility of the sources and cross-reference information when possible.

Data Analysis and Visualization Tools

Data analysis and visualization tools empower journalists to make sense of complex datasets and communicate their findings effectively. Some essential tools and techniques include:

- **Spreadsheet Software:** Programs like Microsoft Excel and Google Sheets are commonly used for data analysis and basic visualization.

- **Data Visualization Tools:** Specialized data visualization tools, such as Tableau and Datawrapper, enable journalists to create compelling charts, graphs, and interactive visualizations.

- **Statistical Software:** Statistical software packages like R and Python with libraries like pandas and matplotlib are invaluable for in-depth data analysis and advanced visualization.

- **Geospatial Tools:** Geospatial software, including Geographic Information Systems (GIS) software, allows journalists to map and analyze location-based data.

- **Machine Learning and AI:** Advanced data journalism may involve machine learning and AI algorithms for predictive analysis or uncovering patterns in large datasets.

Open Data Initiatives

Many governments and organizations participate in open data initiatives, making a wealth of data freely accessible to the public. Open data portals provide journalists with a rich source of information for investigative reporting and analysis. These initiatives promote transparency and empower journalists to hold institutions accountable.

Data Journalism Communities

Data journalism is a collaborative field, and journalists often collaborate with data scientists, programmers, and domain experts. Online communities and forums dedicated to data journalism provide opportunities for learning, sharing, and seeking assistance with data-related challenges.

In the subsequent pages of this chapter, we will explore these data sources and tools in greater detail, providing practical guidance, examples, and case studies. Whether you're a novice or an experienced data journalist, understanding how to access, analyze, and visualize data is essential for leveraging its potential in your storytelling.

Creating Compelling Data Visualizations

The Power of Data Visualization

Data journalism is not just about collecting and analyzing data; it's also about effectively communicating the insights and stories found within the data. Data visualizations play a crucial role in making complex information accessible, engaging, and memorable. Here, we explore the art and science of creating compelling data visualizations.

Types of Data Visualizations

Data journalists have a range of visualization options at their disposal, each suited to specific data types and storytelling goals:

- **Bar Charts and Histograms:** These are suitable for comparing categories or showing distribution patterns within a dataset. For example, a bar chart could illustrate the popularity of different smartphone brands among consumers.

- **Line Charts:** Line charts are excellent for displaying trends over time, such as stock market fluctuations, temperature changes, or demographic shifts.

- **Pie Charts:** While often debated for their effectiveness, pie charts can be useful for showing parts of a whole, such as the composition of a budget or the share of market sectors.

- **Scatter Plots:** Scatter plots reveal relationships between two variables. They are helpful for identifying correlations or outliers in data.

- **Maps and Geospatial Visualizations:** These are ideal for displaying data with a geographical component, like population density, election results by region, or environmental data.

- **Interactive Visualizations:** Interactive visualizations, including interactive maps and charts, allow readers to explore data on their own. They are particularly useful for online articles and reports.

Design Principles for Data Visualizations

Effective data visualizations adhere to design principles that enhance clarity and understanding:

- **Simplicity:** Keep visualizations clean and uncluttered. Avoid unnecessary decorations or embellishments.

- **Labeling:** Clearly label axes, data points, and any relevant information. Labels should be concise and easy to read.

- **Color Choices:** Use color strategically to highlight key points or categories. Ensure that color choices are accessible to all readers, including those with color vision deficiencies.

- **Consistency:** Maintain consistent design elements throughout your visualizations to provide a cohesive reading experience.

- **Narrative Flow:** Visualizations should complement the narrative of the story. They should enhance the reader's understanding of the data, not confuse them.

Tools for Creating Data Visualizations

Several tools and software options are available for creating data visualizations, catering to various skill levels and needs:

- **Data Visualization Libraries:** Libraries like D3.js (Data-Driven Documents), Chart.js, and Highcharts are popular among developers for creating custom interactive visualizations.

- **Data Visualization Software:** Tools like Tableau, Microsoft Power BI, and Google Data Studio provide user-friendly interfaces for designing and sharing visualizations.

- **Programming Languages:** If you have coding experience, languages like R and Python offer libraries and packages for data visualization, such as ggplot2 and matplotlib.

- **Online Visualization Platforms:** Online platforms like Infogram and Canva offer pre-designed templates and drag-and-drop interfaces for creating quick visualizations.

Storytelling with Data Visualizations

Data visualizations should serve a storytelling purpose. They should enhance the narrative, clarify complex concepts, and provide readers with meaningful insights. When incorporating visualizations into your journalism, consider the following:

- **Context:** Provide context and explanations alongside visualizations to guide readers in understanding what they see.

- **Interactivity:** When appropriate, allow readers to interact with the data, explore different aspects, or view underlying details.

- **Annotations:** Use annotations, captions, or callouts to draw attention to specific data points or trends within the visualization.

- **Comparisons:** Visualizations are excellent for showing comparisons between data points, groups, or time periods. Make these comparisons clear and relevant to the story.

Chapter 8: Tools and Resources for Internet Journalism

Essential Websites for Journalists

In the digital age, journalists have access to a wealth of online resources that can streamline their research, fact-checking, and reporting processes. This section highlights essential websites and online tools that journalists can leverage to enhance their work.

1. ProPublica

ProPublica is an independent, nonprofit newsroom dedicated to investigative journalism. Their website offers a treasure trove of investigative reports, data sets, and resources that journalists can use as references and inspiration for their own stories. ProPublica's commitment to transparency and high-quality journalism makes it a valuable resource for investigative reporters.

2. Poynter

Poynter is a renowned organization focused on journalism education and ethics. Their website provides a wide range of resources, including training materials, articles, and tools that help journalists enhance their skills and stay updated on industry trends. Poynter's fact-checking resources are particularly valuable in an era where misinformation is prevalent.

3. Google News Lab

Google News Lab offers a suite of tools and resources for journalists. From Google Trends for tracking the popularity of search terms to Google Earth for visualizing geographic data, these tools empower journalists to uncover stories and present them in engaging ways. The News Lab also provides training materials and case studies to help journalists make the most of Google's tools.

4. Data.gov

Data.gov is the United States government's open data portal. It provides access to a vast array of government datasets on topics ranging from economics and healthcare to climate and education. Journalists can use these datasets for in-depth reporting and analysis. The portal also includes tools for data visualization and exploration.

5. Snopes

Snopes is a fact-checking website known for debunking myths, rumors, and urban legends. Journalists can use Snopes as a quick reference to verify the accuracy of viral claims and widely circulated stories. It's a valuable resource for maintaining credibility in reporting.

6. Columbia Journalism Review

The Columbia Journalism Review (CJR) is a publication that focuses on media criticism and analysis. Their website features in-depth articles and reports on journalism ethics, media trends, and industry developments. Journalists can gain valuable insights into the challenges and opportunities facing the field of journalism.

7. Storybench

Storybench is a digital publication dedicated to showcasing innovative approaches to storytelling in journalism. It provides case studies, tutorials, and examples of data-driven and multimedia storytelling techniques. Journalists can draw inspiration from Storybench to create engaging and impactful narratives.

8. Internet Archive

The Internet Archive is a vast digital library that captures and preserves web content over time. Journalists can use it to access historical versions of websites, news articles, and multimedia content. This resource is invaluable for researching past events and tracking the evolution of online narratives.

9. Reporters Committee for Freedom of the Press

The Reporters Committee for Freedom of the Press is an organization dedicated to defending the First Amendment and supporting the rights of journalists. Their website offers legal resources, guides, and tools to help journalists navigate legal challenges and access public information.

10. Journo Portfolio

Journo Portfolio is a platform that allows journalists to create and showcase their online portfolios. It's an essential tool for journalists looking to establish a professional online presence, showcase their work, and connect with potential employers or freelance opportunities.

11. Media Bias/Fact Check

Media Bias/Fact Check is a website that evaluates the bias and fact-checking accuracy of news sources. Journalists can use this resource to assess the credibility of news outlets and sources they plan to reference in their reporting.

In the rapidly evolving landscape of internet journalism, staying informed and leveraging digital tools is crucial. These essential websites offer a starting point for journalists to access valuable information, fact-check claims, enhance their skills, and uphold the principles of responsible journalism.

Mobile Apps for On-the-Go Reporting

Mobile journalism, often referred to as "mojo," has become a prominent aspect of modern reporting. Journalists are no longer tethered to newsrooms; they can gather, edit, and publish stories directly from their mobile devices. This section explores essential mobile apps that empower journalists for on-the-go reporting.

1. FiLMiC Pro

FiLMiC Pro is a high-quality video recording app for smartphones. It provides manual control over focus, exposure, and white balance, allowing journalists to capture professional-grade video footage. This app is particularly useful for on-the-spot interviews, live reporting, and documentary-style storytelling.

2. <u>Voice Record Pro</u>

Voice Record Pro is a versatile audio recording app that enables journalists to capture high-quality audio interviews and ambient sound. It offers features like audio editing, cloud storage integration, and the ability to add markers during recordings for easy reference.

3. <u>Evernote</u>

Evernote is a note-taking app that helps journalists organize their research, interview notes, and story ideas. Its cross-platform compatibility ensures that notes are accessible on both mobile devices and computers, making it a valuable tool for seamless information management.

4. <u>CamScanner</u>

CamScanner allows journalists to quickly scan documents, receipts, or handwritten notes using their mobile device's camera. The app converts these scans into high-quality PDFs, making it easier to digitize and store important documents while on assignment.

5. <u>TapeACall</u>

TapeACall is a call recording app that can be invaluable for conducting and transcribing phone interviews. It offers both manual and automatic recording options, ensuring that interviews are captured accurately.

6. iMovie

iMovie is a video editing app for iOS devices. Journalists can use it to edit and enhance their video footage, add transitions, text overlays, and even create basic animations. It's an accessible and user-friendly tool for producing polished video content on the go.

7. Snapseed and Adobe Lightroom Mobile

Snapseed and Adobe Lightroom Mobile are powerful photo editing apps. They provide a wide range of editing options, including exposure adjustments, color correction, and filters. Journalists can use these apps to enhance the visual quality of their photos before publishing.

8. Ulysses

Ulysses is a writing app for journalists who prefer a distraction-free environment for writing and note-taking. It offers features like Markdown support, document organization, and seamless synchronization across devices.

9. TweetDeck

For journalists who use Twitter as a reporting tool, TweetDeck offers advanced features for managing multiple Twitter accounts, tracking specific hashtags, and monitoring real-time updates. It simplifies social media monitoring while on the move.

10. Signal

Signal is an encrypted messaging app known for its security features. Journalists can use it to communicate securely with sources, colleagues, and editors when handling sensitive stories or protecting the confidentiality of their sources.

11. Scanner Radio and Police Scanner

Scanner Radio and Police Scanner apps provide real-time access to police, fire, and emergency scanner feeds. They can be invaluable for staying informed about breaking news and events in your area, enabling reporters to respond quickly to developing stories.

These mobile apps are essential tools for journalists who need to capture, edit, and disseminate news while on the go. They empower reporters to be more flexible, agile, and efficient in their reporting endeavors. Whether you're covering a live event, conducting interviews, or documenting breaking news, these apps can significantly enhance your mobile journalism toolkit.

Must-Follow Blogs and News Aggregators

In the ever-evolving landscape of internet journalism, staying informed about the latest trends, tools, and industry insights is essential for journalists. This section highlights must-follow blogs and news aggregators that provide valuable information, analysis, and inspiration for journalists navigating the digital realm.

1. Nieman Lab

Nieman Lab, affiliated with Harvard University, is a trusted source for news and analysis of journalism and media innovation. It covers topics such as digital storytelling, media ethics, and emerging technologies. Journalists can gain valuable insights into the evolving media landscape from this reputable source.

2. Poynter's MediaWise

Poynter's MediaWise initiative focuses on media literacy and fact-checking. Their blog offers valuable resources and updates on combatting misinformation and improving media literacy skills. For journalists committed to responsible reporting, this blog is an essential read.

3. Journalism.co.uk

Journalism.co.uk covers a wide range of topics relevant to journalists, including digital journalism techniques, industry trends, and media innovation. The blog offers practical advice, case studies, and interviews with leading journalists and experts.

4. CJR's The Kicker

The Kicker, part of the Columbia Journalism Review (CJR), provides commentary and analysis on the state of journalism. It covers topics such as press freedom, media ethics, and the challenges faced by news organizations. Journalists can gain a deeper understanding of the industry's dynamics from this blog.

5. Journalism.org

The Pew Research Center's Journalism.org offers data-driven insights into the media landscape. It provides research reports, surveys, and analysis on various aspects of journalism, including audience trends, news consumption, and the impact of technology.

6. MediaShift

MediaShift explores the intersection of media, technology, and culture. The blog covers topics such as digital storytelling, media entrepreneurship, and the evolving media business models. Journalists can stay updated on industry shifts and innovative practices.

7. RJI's Futures Lab

The Reynolds Journalism Institute's Futures Lab blog focuses on emerging technologies and trends in journalism. It explores topics like virtual reality, artificial intelligence, and interactive storytelling, providing journalists with insights into the future of the field.

8. Journalist's Resource

Journalist's Resource, affiliated with Harvard Kennedy School's Shorenstein Center, offers research-backed articles and resources for journalists. It covers topics like data journalism, media ethics, and evidence-based reporting.

9. Mediaite

Mediaite provides coverage and analysis of the media industry, including news organizations, journalists, and media figures. It offers a comprehensive view of media trends, controversies, and developments.

10. Muck Rack Blog

Muck Rack is a platform for journalists and PR professionals. Their blog covers topics relevant to journalists, including media relations, social media best practices, and industry insights. Journalists can find valuable tips and resources for building their online presence.

11. TechCrunch

TechCrunch's media section offers coverage of technology's impact on media and journalism. It explores topics like digital media startups, media tech trends, and innovations in storytelling.

12. Reddit's r/Journalism

Reddit's journalism community provides a forum for journalists to discuss industry news, share resources, and seek advice from peers. It's a valuable source of crowd-sourced insights and discussions.

13. Feedly

Feedly is a versatile news aggregator that allows journalists to curate their own personalized news feeds. It enables them to stay updated on a wide range of topics, including industry news, technology, and media trends.

14. Flipboard

Flipboard is a popular news aggregator app that allows journalists to create customized digital magazines based on their interests. It provides a visually engaging way to consume and share news and industry insights.

15. NewsNow

NewsNow is a news aggregator that offers a wide range of news topics, including journalism and media. Journalists can use it to discover breaking news, trends, and articles from various sources.

These must-follow blogs and news aggregators serve as valuable resources for journalists looking to stay informed, improve their skills, and navigate the ever-evolving world of internet journalism. Whether you're seeking industry analysis, practical tips, or inspiration for your reporting, these sources offer a wealth of knowledge and insights.

Chapter 9: Case Studies in Internet Journalism

In-depth Analysis of Successful Online News Stories

The digital age has ushered in a new era of journalism, one characterized by rapid information dissemination and dynamic storytelling. In this section, we'll embark on an in-depth analysis of successful online news stories to uncover the strategies, techniques, and innovations that have driven their impact and resonance.

1. The New York Times - "The Daily 360"
"The Daily 360" by The New York Times is a groundbreaking series that leverages immersive 360-degree video storytelling. This innovation allows readers to step into the shoes of journalists and experience news events firsthand. The success of "The Daily 360" lies in its ability to engage audiences on a visceral level, making them active participants in the news.

Key Takeaways:

- Immersive experiences enhance audience engagement.

- Innovative use of technology can transform news consumption.

2. ProPublica - "Lost Mothers"
ProPublica's "Lost Mothers" is an investigative series that delves into the maternal mortality crisis in the United States. This project combines in-depth reporting, data analysis, and storytelling to shed light on a critical public health issue. By presenting data in a

compelling narrative, "Lost Mothers" demonstrates the power of data journalism to drive awareness and change.

Key Takeaways:

- Data-driven storytelling can raise awareness of important issues.

- Investigative reporting can drive social change.

3. The Guardian - "The Counted"

"The Counted" by The Guardian is an extensive database and reporting project that tracks police killings in the United States. Through meticulous data collection and visualization, this series provides transparency and accountability in an area where official data was lacking. "The Counted" showcases the power of data journalism to hold institutions accountable.

Key Takeaways:

- Data-driven investigations can fill gaps in official reporting.

- Transparency and accountability are essential in journalism.

4. Vox - "Explained"

Vox's "Explained" series takes complex topics and breaks them down into concise and engaging video explainers. These videos utilize clear graphics, expert interviews, and storytelling to make intricate subjects accessible to a wide audience. "Explained" highlights the value of explanatory journalism in a digital age marked by information overload.

Key Takeaways:

- Explanatory journalism simplifies complex topics.

- Visual storytelling can enhance understanding.

5. BBC - "Africa Eye"

"Africa Eye" by the BBC is an investigative series that combines traditional journalism with digital tools and open-source intelligence. The series exposes human rights abuses, corruption, and environmental issues across Africa. "Africa Eye" demonstrates the potential for cross-border collaboration and digital innovation in investigative journalism.

Key Takeaways:

- Collaboration and technology can transcend geographical boundaries.

- Investigative journalism can amplify underreported stories.

6. The Washington Post - "The Fact Checker"

"The Fact Checker" by The Washington Post is a continuous fact-checking project that critically examines statements made by politicians and public figures. It provides readers with evidence-based analysis and assigns ratings based on the accuracy of claims. "The Fact Checker" showcases the importance of truth and accountability in journalism.

Key Takeaways:

- Fact-checking promotes accuracy and accountability.

- Providing evidence-based analysis can inform public discourse.

7. BuzzFeed News - "The Mueller Report"

BuzzFeed News created an interactive digital version of the Mueller Report, complete with annotations, links, and context. This format made a lengthy government document accessible and engaging to a broad audience. BuzzFeed's approach exemplifies the potential for digital tools to transform traditional reporting materials.

Key Takeaways:

- Digital tools can enhance the accessibility of complex documents.

- Interactivity engages readers in long-form content.

8. The Intercept - "The Drone Papers"

"The Drone Papers" by The Intercept is an investigative series that sheds light on the U.S. drone warfare program. It combines leaked government documents with comprehensive reporting to provide a deep understanding of the program's impact. This series demonstrates the role of investigative journalism in uncovering government secrecy.

Key Takeaways:

- Leaked documents can reveal hidden truths.

- Investigative journalism can challenge government secrecy.

These case studies offer insights into the diverse approaches and techniques that have made online news stories successful in the digital age. From immersive storytelling to data-driven investigations and fact-checking initiatives, these examples showcase the innovative and impactful possibilities of internet journalism.

Lessons Learned from High-Impact Internet Journalism

The world of internet journalism is ever-evolving, and from the successes of high-impact stories, we can distill valuable lessons. In this section, we'll explore the key takeaways and insights that journalists can glean from these exemplary cases.

1. Embrace Multimedia Storytelling

High-impact internet journalism often relies on a combination of text, images, videos, and interactive elements. Embracing multimedia storytelling allows journalists to engage a broader audience. It's not enough to present information; it must be presented in a format that resonates with the digital audience. Whether it's immersive 360-degree videos, interactive data visualizations, or compelling photo essays, multimedia elements enhance the storytelling experience.

Example: The New York Times' "The Daily 360" series demonstrates how immersive video storytelling can captivate audiences and bring them closer to the news.

2. Harness the Power of Data

Data journalism is a formidable tool for uncovering hidden truths and revealing patterns. High-impact stories often involve in-depth data analysis. Journalists should be skilled in collecting, analyzing, and visualizing data to support their narratives. Data-driven storytelling not only provides evidence but also adds a layer of transparency and credibility to reporting.

Example: The Guardian's "The Counted" database showcases the power of data journalism in tracking and reporting on police killings in the United States.

3. Prioritize Investigative Reporting

Investigative journalism remains a cornerstone of high-impact reporting. It involves digging deep into stories, often uncovering hidden information or exposing wrongdoing. Journalists should be persistent, thorough, and unafraid to challenge powerful institutions. Investigative stories can spark conversations, influence policy changes, and hold those in power accountable.

Example: The Intercept's "The Drone Papers" exemplifies the impact of investigative journalism in revealing government secrecy and the consequences of drone warfare.

4. Fact-Check and Verify Information

The proliferation of misinformation in the digital age underscores the importance of fact-checking and verification. High-impact journalism demands accuracy and reliability. Journalists must rigorously fact-check claims, cross-reference sources, and cite credible information. In a time when false information can spread rapidly, the role of the journalist as a truth verifier is critical.

Example: The Washington Post's "The Fact Checker" project provides evidence-based analysis and fact-checking of statements made by politicians and public figures.

5. Engage the Audience Actively

Audience engagement is a two-way street. High-impact journalism involves actively involving the audience. This can be achieved through interactive elements, user-generated content, or crowdsourcing. Journalists should invite readers to participate in discussions, share their experiences, or contribute to investigations. Engaging the audience fosters a sense of ownership and community around the news.

Example: BuzzFeed News' interactive digital version of the Mueller Report invites readers to explore and understand a complex government document actively.

6. Transparency and Accountability Matter

In high-impact journalism, transparency about sources, methods, and intentions is paramount. Journalists should be transparent about their biases and conflicts of interest. Accountability goes beyond holding others responsible; it also means holding oneself accountable. When errors are made, journalists should promptly correct them. Transparency and accountability build trust with the audience.

Example: ProPublica's "Lost Mothers" series demonstrates a commitment to transparency by sharing the methodology behind its maternal mortality investigation.

7. Leverage Digital Tools and Innovations

The digital landscape offers an array of tools and innovations that can enhance storytelling. Journalists should be open to experimenting with new technologies, from virtual reality and augmented reality to data visualization tools and content management systems. Embracing innovation allows for fresh and engaging storytelling formats.

Example: Vox's "Explained" series utilizes clear graphics, animations, and expert interviews to simplify complex topics and make them accessible.

8. Collaborate and Share Resources

Collaboration can amplify the impact of journalism. High-impact stories often involve partnerships between news organizations, nonprofits, or academic institutions. Collaborations enable journalists to pool resources, access expertise, and reach wider audiences. Sharing resources, data, and findings contributes to a culture of collective knowledge.

Example: The BBC's "Africa Eye" series is a testament to cross-border collaboration and the use of open-source intelligence in investigative reporting.

9. Stay Ethical in Reporting

Ethical journalism is the foundation of trust. Journalists should adhere to ethical standards in their reporting, including accuracy, fairness, and respect for privacy. In the face of misinformation, maintaining ethical standards is crucial to preserving the credibility and integrity of journalism.

Example: Maintaining ethical reporting standards is a recurring theme in high-impact stories, ensuring that accuracy is not compromised amid the rush to publish.

10. Engage with the Community

Journalists should actively engage with the communities they serve. This involves listening to readers, responding to their concerns, and being present on social media. Building a sense of community around journalism fosters trust and encourages dialogue.

Example: Reddit's r/Journalism community provides a forum for journalists to engage with peers and discuss industry news and issues.

High-impact internet journalism is a dynamic and evolving field. Learning from successful cases not only inspires journalists but also provides a roadmap for creating meaningful and influential stories in the digital age.

Diverse Examples Across News Categories

Internet journalism encompasses a wide spectrum of news categories, each with its unique challenges and opportunities. In this section, we'll explore diverse examples that span various news categories, shedding light on the versatility of online reporting.

1. Political Reporting - Politico's "POLITICO Playbook" "POLITICO Playbook" by Politico is a daily newsletter that provides a comprehensive roundup of political news and analysis. It serves as a vital resource for political insiders, policymakers, and the general public. The success of this political reporting exemplifies the demand for timely and authoritative coverage in the digital age.

2. Science Journalism - National Geographic's "Planet or Plastic?"

National Geographic's "Planet or Plastic?" is an immersive and interactive project that explores the global plastic pollution crisis. Through stunning visuals, data-driven narratives, and in-depth reporting, it raises awareness about the environmental impact of plastic waste. This project demonstrates the power of science journalism to engage audiences in critical issues.

3. Entertainment Reporting - E! News

E! News is a prominent source for entertainment reporting in the digital realm. It covers celebrity news, pop culture, and entertainment events. E! News showcases how online platforms can cater to a global audience's appetite for entertainment stories and celebrity updates.

4. Technology Journalism - The Verge

The Verge is a leading technology news website that covers the latest trends in the tech industry. With its in-depth articles, reviews, and video content, it provides tech enthusiasts and professionals with valuable insights into the ever-evolving world of technology.

5. Health Reporting - WebMD

WebMD is a trusted source for health information and reporting. It offers a vast repository of articles, expert advice, and resources on various health topics. WebMD illustrates how online platforms can disseminate accurate and accessible health information to a broad audience.

6. Business Journalism - Bloomberg

Bloomberg is a global leader in business and financial journalism. It provides real-time news, market analysis, and insights into the world of finance, economics, and business. Bloomberg's digital platform showcases the power of data-driven reporting in the business sector.

7. Local News - Patch

Patch is a hyperlocal news platform that covers communities across the United States. It offers a mix of news, events, and community updates tailored to specific regions. Patch highlights the importance of online platforms in revitalizing local news coverage.

8. Sports Journalism - ESPN

ESPN is a prominent sports news outlet with a strong online presence. It covers a wide range of sports, providing fans with the latest scores, highlights, and analysis. ESPN showcases how digital platforms cater to the global sports audience's hunger for news and updates.

9. Travel Reporting - Lonely Planet

Lonely Planet is a renowned travel resource that offers travel guides, articles, and destination information. It inspires travelers and provides practical advice for exploring the world. Lonely Planet's digital platform demonstrates the role of online resources in the travel and tourism sector.

10. Opinion and Commentary - The Atlantic's "Ideas"
The Atlantic's "Ideas" section features opinion pieces, essays, and commentary on a wide range of topics. It provides a platform for thought-provoking discussions and diverse perspectives. This section underscores the significance of online platforms in facilitating informed discourse.

These diverse examples across news categories illustrate the breadth and depth of internet journalism. From political reporting and science journalism to entertainment news and local coverage, online platforms have transformed how news is produced, consumed, and shared. The digital age has democratized access to information, allowing journalists to reach global audiences with timely and relevant stories.

Chapter 10: Common Mistakes in Online Reporting

Identifying and Avoiding Errors in Internet Journalism

1. Rushing to Publish

One of the most common errors in online reporting is the rush to publish breaking news. While timeliness is crucial, sacrificing accuracy for speed can lead to misinformation. Journalists should aim to verify facts, cross-reference sources, and confirm details before hitting the publish button.

Example: In the race to report on a breaking news event, a news outlet may publish unverified information, causing confusion and harm.

2. Lack of Source Verification

Failing to verify sources can be a grave mistake. Online journalists should confirm the credibility of their sources, check for bias, and ensure the accuracy of quotes and statements. Relying on unverified or anonymous sources can erode trust in reporting.

Example: A news story citing an anonymous source may lack credibility, and readers may question its accuracy.

3. Falling for Misinformation

Journalists must be vigilant in identifying and debunking misinformation. The digital landscape is rife with false claims and rumors. Fact-checking and verifying information are essential practices to prevent the spread of fake news.

Example: A journalist reporting on a viral social media post without fact-checking may inadvertently amplify false information.

4. Ignoring Ethical Considerations

Ethical lapses can damage a journalist's reputation and harm the public's trust. Online journalists should adhere to ethical guidelines, including accuracy, fairness, and respect for privacy. Correcting errors promptly and transparently is an ethical obligation.

Example: Failing to seek permission before using someone's personal photos in a news story can lead to ethical violations.

5. Lack of Context and Depth

Online reporting can sometimes prioritize brevity over depth. Providing context and background information is crucial to help readers fully understand complex issues. Superficial reporting can lead to misunderstandings.

Example: A news article on a complex geopolitical conflict that lacks historical context may oversimplify the issue.

6. Plagiarism and Uncredited Content

Copying content from other sources without proper attribution is a serious offense. Plagiarism erodes trust and can lead to legal consequences. Journalists should always credit their sources and use quotations for verbatim text.

Example: A journalist copying paragraphs from another article without giving credit may face allegations of plagiarism.

7. Failing to Update or Correct

When errors are discovered, failing to update or correct the article promptly is another common mistake. Journalists should acknowledge and rectify errors transparently, maintaining the credibility of their reporting.

Example: An article with a factual error that remains uncorrected may undermine the news outlet's reputation.

8. Overreliance on Social Media

While social media can be a valuable source of information, overreliance on it without proper verification can lead to errors. Journalists should use social media as a starting point for stories but confirm facts independently.

Example: Reporting on a trending topic on social media without fact-checking may result in inaccuracies.

9. Failure to Engage with the Audience

Ignoring audience feedback and failing to engage with readers can isolate journalists from their readership. Engaging with comments, questions, and feedback fosters a sense of community and accountability.

Example: A journalist who doesn't respond to reader comments may miss opportunities to clarify or correct information.

10. Inadequate Training

Journalists need continuous training to keep up with evolving digital tools and reporting techniques. Inadequate training can lead to errors related to technology, data, and online security.

Example: Journalists lacking data analysis skills may misinterpret statistics in a report, leading to inaccurate reporting.

Identifying and avoiding these common mistakes is essential for upholding the integrity and credibility of internet journalism. By prioritizing accuracy, transparency, and ethical reporting practices, journalists can navigate the challenges of the digital era effectively.

Ethical Pitfalls and How to Steer Clear

1. Rushing to Publish

One of the most common errors in online reporting is the rush to publish breaking news. While timeliness is crucial, sacrificing accuracy for speed can lead to misinformation. Journalists should aim to verify facts, cross-reference sources, and confirm details before hitting the publish button.

Example: In the race to report on a breaking news event, a news outlet may publish unverified information, causing confusion and harm.

2. Lack of Source Verification

Failing to verify sources can be a grave mistake. Online journalists should confirm the credibility of their sources, check for bias, and ensure the accuracy of quotes and statements. Relying on unverified or anonymous sources can erode trust in reporting.

Example: A news story citing an anonymous source may lack credibility, and readers may question its accuracy.

3. Falling for Misinformation

Journalists must be vigilant in identifying and debunking misinformation. The digital landscape is rife with false claims and rumors. Fact-checking and verifying information are essential practices to prevent the spread of fake news.

Example: A journalist reporting on a viral social media post without fact-checking may inadvertently amplify false information.

4. Ignoring Ethical Considerations

Ethical lapses can damage a journalist's reputation and harm the public's trust. Online journalists should adhere to ethical guidelines, including accuracy, fairness, and respect for privacy. Correcting errors promptly and transparently is an ethical obligation.

Example: Failing to seek permission before using someone's personal photos in a news story can lead to ethical violations.

5. Lack of Context and Depth

Online reporting can sometimes prioritize brevity over depth. Providing context and background information is crucial to help readers fully understand complex issues. Superficial reporting can lead to misunderstandings.

Example: A news article on a complex geopolitical conflict that lacks historical context may oversimplify the issue.

6. Plagiarism and Uncredited Content

Copying content from other sources without proper attribution is a serious offense. Plagiarism erodes trust and can lead to legal consequences. Journalists should always credit their sources and use quotations for verbatim text.

Example: A journalist copying paragraphs from another article without giving credit may face allegations of plagiarism.

7. Failing to Update or Correct

When errors are discovered, failing to update or correct the article promptly is another common mistake. Journalists should acknowledge and rectify errors transparently, maintaining the credibility of their reporting.

Example: An article with a factual error that remains uncorrected may undermine the news outlet's reputation.

8. Overreliance on Social Media

While social media can be a valuable source of information, overreliance on it without proper verification can lead to errors. Journalists should use social media as a starting point for stories but confirm facts independently.

Example: Reporting on a trending topic on social media without fact-checking may result in inaccuracies.

9. Failure to Engage with the Audience

Ignoring audience feedback and failing to engage with readers can isolate journalists from their readership. Engaging with comments, questions, and feedback fosters a sense of community and accountability.

Example: A journalist who doesn't respond to reader comments may miss opportunities to clarify or correct information.

10. Inadequate Training

Journalists need continuous training to keep up with evolving digital tools and reporting techniques. Inadequate training can lead to errors related to technology, data, and online security.

Example: Journalists lacking data analysis skills may misinterpret statistics in a report, leading to inaccurate reporting.

11. Ethical Pitfalls and How to Steer Clear

Ethical considerations are at the core of responsible journalism. Journalists must navigate a myriad of ethical challenges in the digital age. Here are some common ethical pitfalls and guidance on how to avoid them:

a. Privacy Concerns

- Pitfall: Invading an individual's privacy without just cause.

- Solution: Respect privacy rights and obtain consent when necessary.

b. Conflicts of Interest

- Pitfall: Allowing personal interests or relationships to compromise objectivity.

- Solution: Disclose conflicts of interest and recuse oneself when necessary.

c. Sensationalism

- Pitfall: Prioritizing sensational stories over substantive reporting.

- Solution: Focus on accuracy, balance, and responsible reporting.

d. Clickbait Headlines

- Pitfall: Using misleading or sensational headlines to attract clicks.

- Solution: Craft honest and informative headlines that accurately represent the content.

e. Social Media Conduct

- Pitfall: Engaging in offensive or unprofessional behavior on social media.

- Solution: Maintain professionalism and respect when using social media as a journalist.

f. Handling User-Generated Content

- Pitfall: Sharing user-generated content without verifying authenticity.

- Solution: Verify the source and authenticity of user-generated content before use.

g. Transparent Corrections

- Pitfall: Failing to correct errors promptly and transparently.

- Solution: Acknowledge errors, correct them, and provide clear explanations.

Ethical journalism is the foundation of trust between journalists and their audience. By recognizing and avoiding these ethical pitfalls, journalists can uphold their commitment to accurate, fair, and responsible reporting.

Handling Online Criticism and Controversies

1. Rushing to Publish

One of the most common errors in online reporting is the rush to publish breaking news. While timeliness is crucial, sacrificing accuracy for speed can lead to misinformation. Journalists should aim to verify facts, cross-reference sources, and confirm details before hitting the publish button.

Example: In the race to report on a breaking news event, a news outlet may publish unverified information, causing confusion and harm.

2. Lack of Source Verification

Failing to verify sources can be a grave mistake. Online journalists should confirm the credibility of their sources, check for bias, and ensure the accuracy of quotes and statements. Relying on unverified or anonymous sources can erode trust in reporting.

Example: A news story citing an anonymous source may lack credibility, and readers may question its accuracy.

3. Falling for Misinformation

Journalists must be vigilant in identifying and debunking misinformation. The digital landscape is rife with false claims and rumors. Fact-checking and verifying information are essential practices to prevent the spread of fake news.

Example: A journalist reporting on a viral social media post without fact-checking may inadvertently amplify false information.

4. Ignoring Ethical Considerations

Ethical lapses can damage a journalist's reputation and harm the public's trust. Online journalists should adhere to ethical guidelines, including accuracy, fairness, and respect for privacy. Correcting errors promptly and transparently is an ethical obligation.

Example: Failing to seek permission before using someone's personal photos in a news story can lead to ethical violations.

5. Lack of Context and Depth

Online reporting can sometimes prioritize brevity over depth. Providing context and background information is crucial to help readers fully understand complex issues. Superficial reporting can lead to misunderstandings.

Example: A news article on a complex geopolitical conflict that lacks historical context may oversimplify the issue.

6. Plagiarism and Uncredited Content

Copying content from other sources without proper attribution is a serious offense. Plagiarism erodes trust and can lead to legal consequences. Journalists should always credit their sources and use quotations for verbatim text.

Example: A journalist copying paragraphs from another article without giving credit may face allegations of plagiarism.

7. Failing to Update or Correct

When errors are discovered, failing to update or correct the article promptly is another common mistake. Journalists should acknowledge and rectify errors transparently, maintaining the credibility of their reporting.

Example: An article with a factual error that remains uncorrected may undermine the news outlet's reputation.

8. Overreliance on Social Media

While social media can be a valuable source of information, overreliance on it without proper verification can lead to errors. Journalists should use social media as a starting point for stories but confirm facts independently.

Example: Reporting on a trending topic on social media without fact-checking may result in inaccuracies.

9. Failure to Engage with the Audience

Ignoring audience feedback and failing to engage with readers can isolate journalists from their readership. Engaging with comments, questions, and feedback fosters a sense of community and accountability.

Example: A journalist who doesn't respond to reader comments may miss opportunities to clarify or correct information.

10. Inadequate Training

Journalists need continuous training to keep up with evolving digital tools and reporting techniques. Inadequate training can lead to errors related to technology, data, and online security.

Example: Journalists lacking data analysis skills may misinterpret statistics in a report, leading to inaccurate reporting.

11. Handling Online Criticism and Controversies

Navigating online criticism and controversies is an inevitable aspect of internet journalism. Here are strategies to handle such situations effectively:

a. Maintain Professionalism

- Pitfall: Reacting emotionally to criticism.

- Solution: Respond calmly and professionally, addressing valid points.

b. Fact-Based Responses

- Pitfall: Responding with subjective opinions.

- Solution: Provide evidence-based responses, reinforcing the accuracy of your reporting.

c. Engage Constructively

- Pitfall: Ignoring or dismissing valid criticism.

- Solution: Engage in constructive dialogues, acknowledging areas for improvement.

d. Transparency

- Pitfall: Failing to explain editorial decisions.

- Solution: Be transparent about editorial choices and corrections.

e. Learn and Adapt

- Pitfall: Repeating the same mistakes.

- Solution: Learn from feedback and controversies, and implement improvements.

Handling online criticism and controversies with professionalism and transparency can help journalists maintain credibility and public trust, even in challenging situations.

Chapter 11: Tips for Aspiring Internet Journalists

Building a Strong Online Presence as a Journalist

Establishing a robust online presence is essential for modern journalists. It not only helps in reaching a wider audience but also builds credibility and trust. Here are strategies for building and maintaining a strong online presence:

1. Creating a Professional Website

- Why It Matters: A professional website serves as your online portfolio and resume. It's a centralized hub for your work, background, and contact information.

- Key Steps:

- Register a domain name that reflects your name or brand.

- Design an easy-to-navigate website with a clean layout.

- Showcase your best work, including articles, videos, and multimedia projects.

- Include a bio, resume, and contact information for inquiries and collaborations.

2. Active Social Media Engagement

- Why It Matters: Social media platforms are vital for connecting with your audience, sharing your work, and staying updated on trends.

- Key Steps:

- Choose platforms relevant to your niche (e.g., Twitter, LinkedIn, Instagram).

- Maintain consistency in posting, engaging with followers, and sharing valuable content.

- Use appropriate hashtags to increase the discoverability of your posts.

- Share not only your work but also insights, opinions, and industry news.

3. Blogging and Guest Posting

- Why It Matters: Blogging allows you to express your expertise and engage with a niche audience. Guest posting on reputable websites expands your reach.

- Key Steps:

- Start a blog on your website to discuss topics related to your field.

- Guest post on established platforms to tap into their audience.

- Write thought-provoking, informative, and well-researched articles.

- Provide valuable insights and solutions to readers' questions.

4. Networking and Collaboration

- **Why It Matters:** Building relationships within the industry can lead to opportunities, collaborations, and mentorship.

- **Key Steps:**

- Attend industry events, conferences, and webinars.

- Join online forums, discussion groups, and LinkedIn communities.

- Reach out to professionals for informational interviews and mentorship.

- Collaborate with peers on projects or co-authored articles.

5. Online Portfolios and Multimedia

- **Why It Matters:** Showcasing a diverse range of multimedia content can attract a broader audience.

- **Key Steps:**

- Create multimedia content, such as podcasts, videos, and infographics.

- Host your content on platforms like YouTube, SoundCloud, or Vimeo.

- Share snippets and teasers on social media to pique interest.

- Highlight your multimedia work on your website.

6. Consistent Personal Branding

- **Why It Matters:** A consistent personal brand helps you stand out and builds trust with your audience.

- **Key Steps:**

- Develop a unique style, voice, and tone that align with your niche.

- Use a consistent profile picture and cover photo across all platforms.

- Craft a compelling bio that communicates your expertise and interests.

- Maintain a consistent posting schedule to keep your audience engaged.

7. Engaging with Your Audience

- **Why It Matters:** Engaging with your audience fosters a sense of community and loyalty.

- **Key Steps:**

- Respond promptly to comments, messages, and questions.

- Host Q&A sessions, live streams, or webinars to interact with your audience in real-time.

- Encourage discussions and debates on relevant topics.

- Show appreciation for your followers' support and feedback.

8. Monitoring and Adapting

- **Why It Matters:** The digital landscape is dynamic. Monitoring your online presence and adapting to changes is crucial.

- **Key Steps:**

- Use analytics tools to track the performance of your content and social media engagement.

- Pay attention to audience feedback and adjust your strategies accordingly.

- Stay updated on industry trends, technology, and emerging platforms.

- Continuously refine your online presence based on what works best.

Building a strong online presence as a journalist is an ongoing process that requires dedication and adaptability. By following these strategies, you can connect with your audience, establish credibility, and advance your career in internet journalism.

Networking and Collaborating in the Digital Space

Networking and collaboration are pillars of success in internet journalism. They enable you to expand your reach, access valuable resources, and learn from others in your field. Here's how to effectively network and collaborate in the digital space:

1. Online Communities and Forums

- **Why They Matter:** Online communities and forums are hubs for like-minded individuals in your niche. They provide a platform for discussions, knowledge sharing, and networking.

- **Key Steps:**

    - Join relevant online communities, such as Reddit subreddits or specialized forums.

    - Participate actively by asking questions, sharing insights, and engaging in discussions.

    - Build your reputation as a knowledgeable and helpful member of the community.

    - Use these platforms to connect with peers and potential collaborators.

2. Social Media Groups

- **Why They Matter:** Many social media platforms have groups or communities centered around specific topics or industries. These groups facilitate networking and collaboration.

- **Key Steps:**

    - Identify and join groups related to your niche on platforms like LinkedIn or Facebook.

- Contribute meaningfully by sharing articles, insights, and participating in discussions.

- Connect with group members who share your interests or have complementary skills.

- Explore collaboration opportunities, such as co-authoring articles or joint projects.

3. Webinars and Virtual Events

- **Why They Matter:** Webinars and virtual events offer opportunities to learn from experts, ask questions, and connect with industry professionals.

- **Key Steps:**

  - Register for webinars, online workshops, and virtual conferences in your field.

  - Attend sessions and actively engage in Q&A sessions or networking breaks.

  - Use event platforms to connect with speakers, panelists, and attendees.

  - Follow up with connections after the event to nurture relationships.

4. LinkedIn Networking

- **Why It Matters:** LinkedIn is a powerful platform for professional networking, allowing you to connect with journalists, editors, and industry leaders.

- **Key Steps:**

- Optimize your LinkedIn profile with a professional photo, detailed summary, and relevant keywords.

- Connect with professionals in your field, including editors, reporters, and influencers.

- Share your work, insights, and articles to showcase your expertise.

- Engage with your network through comments, likes, and shares.

5. Cold Outreach and Informational Interviews

- **Why They Matter:** Proactive outreach can lead to valuable connections and mentorship opportunities.

- **Key Steps:**

  - Identify professionals whose work you admire or who hold positions you aspire to.

  - Reach out with a personalized message expressing your admiration and seeking advice.

  - Request informational interviews to learn from their experiences and insights.

  - Respect their time and maintain a professional demeanor in all interactions.

6. Collaborative Projects

- **Why They Matter:** Collaborative projects, such as co-authored articles or multimedia productions, can leverage the strengths of multiple individuals.

- **Key Steps:**

    - Identify potential collaborators with complementary skills or expertise.

    - Discuss project ideas, goals, and expectations transparently.

    - Establish clear roles and responsibilities for each collaborator.

    - Communicate effectively throughout the project's duration.

7. Professional Organizations

- **Why They Matter:** Joining professional journalism organizations offers networking opportunities, access to resources, and industry insights.

- **Key Steps:**

    - Research and join reputable organizations like the Society of Professional Journalists or Online News Association.

    - Attend their events, conferences, and workshops.

    - Network with fellow members and industry leaders.

    - Take advantage of resources and training provided by the organization.

Networking and collaborating in the digital space are essential for growth and success in internet journalism.

Building meaningful connections and partnerships can open doors to new opportunities, enhance your skills, and enrich your career in the ever-evolving landscape of digital journalism.

Career Paths and Opportunities in Internet Journalism

Establishing a robust online presence is essential for modern journalists. It not only helps in reaching a wider audience but also builds credibility and trust. Here are strategies for building and maintaining a strong online presence:

1. Creating a Professional Website

- **Why It Matters:** A professional website serves as your online portfolio and resume. It's a centralized hub for your work, background, and contact information.

- **Key Steps:**

    - Register a domain name that reflects your name or brand.

    - Design an easy-to-navigate website with a clean layout.

    - Showcase your best work, including articles, videos, and multimedia projects.

    - Include a bio, resume, and contact information for inquiries and collaborations.

2. Active Social Media Engagement

- **Why It Matters:** Social media platforms are vital for connecting with your audience, sharing your work, and staying updated on trends.
- **Key Steps:**
    - Choose platforms relevant to your niche (e.g., Twitter, LinkedIn, Instagram).
    - Maintain consistency in posting, engaging with followers, and sharing valuable content.
    - Use appropriate hashtags to increase the discoverability of your posts.
    - Share not only your work but also insights, opinions, and industry news.

3. Blogging and Guest Posting

- **Why It Matters:** Blogging allows you to express your expertise and engage with a niche audience. Guest posting on reputable websites expands your reach.

- **Key Steps:**
    - Start a blog on your website to discuss topics related to your field.
    - Guest post on established platforms to tap into their audience.
    - Write thought-provoking, informative, and well-researched articles.

- Provide valuable insights and solutions to readers' questions.

4. Networking and Collaboration

- **Why It Matters:** Building relationships within the industry can lead to opportunities, collaborations, and mentorship.

- **Key Steps:**

  - Attend industry events, conferences, and webinars.

  - Join online forums, discussion groups, and LinkedIn communities.

  - Reach out to professionals for informational interviews and mentorship.

  - Collaborate with peers on projects or co-authored articles.

5. Career Paths and Opportunities in Internet Journalism

- **Description:** Internet journalism offers a diverse range of career paths and opportunities, reflecting the evolving nature of the field. Here's an exploration of some key career paths and the opportunities they offer:

  - **Traditional News Outlets:** Cover a wide range of topics or specialize in a particular beat.

- **Digital-First Media:** Produce content primarily for web audiences.

- **Freelance Journalism:** Work independently, contributing to multiple outlets.

- **Blogging and Content Creation:** Build your own platform to share expertise and opinions.

- **Data Journalism and Analytics:** Use data analysis tools and visualization techniques.

- **Social Media and Community Management:** Maintain a brand's online presence.

- **Podcasting and Audio Journalism:** Produce audio content, including news reports.

- **Emerging Technologies:** Explore opportunities in immersive storytelling and AI-driven content.

- **Educational and Training Roles:** Transition into teaching or mentoring roles.

Building a strong online presence as a journalist is an ongoing process that requires dedication and adaptability. By following these strategies and considering various career paths, you can connect with your audience, establish credibility, and advance your career in internet journalism.

Chapter 12: The Future of Internet Journalism

Emerging Trends in Online News

The landscape of internet journalism is constantly evolving, shaped by technological advancements, changing audience behaviors, and the demands of the digital age. In this chapter, we explore the emerging trends in online news that are likely to define the future of journalism:

1. Artificial Intelligence (AI) and Automation

- **The Role of AI:** Artificial intelligence is transforming newsrooms by automating tasks such as content generation, data analysis, and even news reporting. AI-powered algorithms can generate articles, analyze data trends, and provide personalized news recommendations to readers.

- **Enhanced Efficiency:** AI tools enable journalists to focus more on in-depth reporting and analysis while automating routine tasks. This can lead to greater efficiency in news production.

2. Virtual Reality (VR) and Augmented Reality (AR)

- **Immersive Storytelling:** VR and AR technologies are opening up new possibilities for immersive storytelling. Journalists can create virtual environments to transport readers to the heart of a story.

- **Interactive Experiences:** Readers can engage with news stories in ways never before possible. For example, they can explore crime scenes, historical events, or natural disasters through interactive VR experiences.

3. Data Journalism and Visualization

- **Data-Driven Reporting:** Data journalism continues to gain prominence as journalists harness the power of data to uncover stories, analyze trends, and provide informative visuals.

- **Visual Storytelling:** Infographics, interactive charts, and data visualizations make complex information more accessible to readers.

4. Subscription and Membership Models

- **Diversification of Revenue:** News organizations are increasingly adopting subscription and membership models to diversify their revenue streams. Subscribers gain access to premium content and exclusive features.

- **Sustainability:** Subscription models help news outlets reduce their reliance on advertising revenue, potentially leading to more sustainable journalism.

5. Personalization and Recommendation Algorithms

- **Tailored Content:** Recommendation algorithms use reader data to offer personalized news content, increasing reader engagement and loyalty.

- **Ethical Concerns:** The use of algorithms raises ethical questions regarding filter bubbles, bias, and the potential for echo chambers in news consumption.

6. Blockchain Technology and Trust

- **Securing Information:** Blockchain technology is being explored to enhance the security and authenticity of news content. It can help verify the source of information and combat fake news.

- **Transparency:** Blockchain can provide transparent records of edits and revisions to news stories, increasing trust in journalistic integrity.

7. Collaboration and Crowdsourced Journalism

- **Crowdsourced Reporting:** Journalists are increasingly collaborating with readers and citizen journalists to gather information and verify stories. This inclusive approach can lead to a wider range of perspectives.

- **Community Engagement:** Building a community of engaged readers can help news outlets foster trust and gather valuable insights.

8. Ethical Challenges in the Digital Age

- **Deepfakes and Misinformation:** The spread of deepfake technology presents new challenges in verifying the authenticity of video and audio content.

- **Privacy Concerns:** Journalists must navigate ethical dilemmas related to privacy when using data and surveillance technologies in reporting.

The future of internet journalism holds exciting opportunities and complex challenges. As technology continues to advance, journalists must adapt to new tools and storytelling formats while upholding ethical standards. The trends mentioned here represent a glimpse into what lies ahead in the ever-evolving world of online news.

Challenges and Opportunities in a Rapidly Changing Landscape

The fast-paced evolution of internet journalism brings both significant challenges and exciting opportunities to the forefront. Journalists and news organizations must navigate this dynamic landscape to stay relevant, deliver quality content, and maintain the trust of their audiences. Here, we examine the complexities and potential advantages that emerge in this ever-changing environment:

1. Information Overload and Verification

- **Challenge:** The digital age has inundated readers with a vast amount of information, making it challenging to discern credible sources from unreliable ones. The speed at which information spreads can lead to the rapid dissemination of false or misleading content.

- **Opportunity:** Journalists play a crucial role in verifying information and providing context. Fact-checking, source verification, and responsible reporting are key to maintaining credibility.

2. Monetization and Sustainability

- **Challenge:** Traditional advertising models are facing challenges in the digital realm due to ad-blockers and changing consumer behavior. News organizations must find new revenue streams to sustain quality journalism.

- **Opportunity:** Subscription models, memberships, and philanthropic support offer avenues for financial sustainability. Diversifying revenue sources can reduce dependence on advertising.

3. Trust and Ethical Concerns

- **Challenge:** Trust in journalism has been eroded by the proliferation of fake news and sensationalism. Ethical considerations become more complex in the digital age.

- **Opportunity:** Upholding ethical standards, transparency, and accountability can help rebuild trust. Engaging with readers and involving them in the editorial process can foster a sense of transparency and responsibility.

4. Digital Divide and Accessibility

- **Challenge:** Not all populations have equal access to the internet and digital news sources, creating a digital divide. Accessibility issues may limit the reach of online journalism.

- **Opportunity:** Efforts to bridge the digital divide, expand internet access, and provide news in multiple formats can help ensure that journalism reaches a broader audience.

5. Privacy and Data Security

- **Challenge:** Gathering and using data for personalized content raises concerns about privacy and data security. News organizations must handle user data responsibly.

- **Opportunity:** Maintaining strict data security measures and being transparent about data collection practices can build trust with readers while still offering personalized content.

6. Engagement and Community Building

- **Challenge:** Engaging and retaining readers in a digital world saturated with content is a constant challenge. Building a loyal readership base requires ongoing effort.

- **Opportunity:** Creating interactive content, hosting live events, and fostering online communities can enhance reader engagement and loyalty.

7. Regulatory Changes and Press Freedom

- **Challenge:** Evolving regulations on the internet, including issues related to misinformation and content moderation, can pose threats to press freedom and journalistic independence.

- **Opportunity:** Advocating for press freedom, journalistic integrity, and ethical standards remains essential. News organizations can also adapt to changing regulations while upholding their principles.

8. Innovation and Storytelling

- **Challenge:** The digital age demands innovation in storytelling to capture and retain reader attention. Stale or conventional approaches may struggle to compete in the digital landscape.

- **Opportunity:** Embracing new storytelling formats, multimedia content, and emerging technologies like virtual reality and augmented reality can create immersive and captivating news experiences.

9. Global Reach and Cross-Cultural Reporting

- **Challenge:** Internet journalism reaches a global audience, necessitating cross-cultural sensitivity and understanding. Reporting on international issues can be complex.

- **Opportunity:** Diverse perspectives and voices can enrich reporting. Collaborations with journalists from different cultural backgrounds can lead to more comprehensive and accurate coverage.

10. Education and Training

- **Challenge:** Journalists must continually update their skills to keep pace with evolving technologies and trends. Access to quality journalism education is vital.

- **Opportunity:** Educational institutions, news organizations, and online resources offer opportunities for journalists to upskill and adapt to changing demands.

Navigating the rapidly changing landscape of internet journalism is a complex endeavor, but it also presents an array of opportunities for those willing to embrace innovation and uphold the principles of responsible journalism. Adapting to new technologies, engaging with readers, and maintaining ethical standards are all key elements of success in this dynamic field.

Preparing for the Future as an Internet Journalist

As the landscape of journalism continues to transform in the digital age, aspiring internet journalists must equip themselves with a versatile skill set and a forward-thinking mindset. Preparing for the future in this dynamic field requires a blend of traditional journalistic values and adaptability to emerging trends. Here, we delve into the essential steps for individuals looking to thrive as internet journalists in an ever-evolving media landscape:

1. Master the Fundamentals of Journalism

- **Strong Writing Skills:** At the core of journalism is the ability to convey information accurately, concisely, and engagingly. Practice writing in various formats, from news articles to features and op-eds.

- **Critical Thinking:** Develop a sharp eye for spotting misinformation, bias, and gaps in stories. Ask probing questions and verify facts rigorously.

- **Ethical Foundations:** Understand and uphold ethical standards in reporting, including principles such as accuracy, fairness, objectivity, and accountability.

2. Embrace Multimedia Storytelling

- **Versatility:** Equip yourself with multimedia skills, including video production, audio recording, and graphic design. Being proficient in various formats broadens your storytelling capabilities.

- **Visual Literacy:** Learn how to create compelling visuals, such as infographics and data visualizations, to enhance the impact of your stories.

3. Stay Tech-Savvy

- **Digital Tools:** Familiarize yourself with digital tools and software commonly used in newsrooms, including content management systems (CMS), data analysis tools, and social media platforms.

- **Coding and Web Development:** Basic knowledge of HTML, CSS, and web development can be advantageous for journalists working in digital media.

- **Data Analysis:** Develop skills in data analysis and visualization to excel in data journalism, a field with increasing demand.

4. Cultivate a Niche Expertise

- **Choose a Beat:** Specialize in a particular area of interest, whether it's politics, technology, health, or any other field. Becoming an expert in your chosen beat allows you to provide in-depth coverage.

- **Continuous Learning:** Stay updated on developments in your niche through ongoing research, attending conferences, and building a network of experts.

5. Adapt to Emerging Technologies

- **Virtual Reality (VR) and Augmented Reality (AR):** Explore the potential of immersive storytelling through VR and AR technologies. Learn to create immersive experiences that transport readers into your stories.

- **Artificial Intelligence (AI):** Understand how AI can assist in data analysis, content creation, and personalization. Keep an eye on AI developments in journalism.

- **Blockchain and Verification:** Familiarize yourself with blockchain technology for enhancing transparency and verification in reporting.

6. Build an Online Presence

- **Professional Website:** Create a personal website or portfolio showcasing your work, expertise, and contact information. Your website serves as a digital resume and a platform for self-promotion.

- **Social Media Engagement:** Be active on social media platforms relevant to your niche. Share your work, engage with your audience, and build a community of followers.

7. Network and Collaborate

- **Connect with Peers:** Establish relationships with fellow journalists, both online and offline. Networking can lead to collaborations, mentorship, and valuable insights.

- **Collaborative Projects:** Collaborate with experts, photographers, videographers, and data analysts to produce comprehensive multimedia stories.

8. Adapt to New Business Models

- **Diversify Income:** Explore various revenue streams such as freelance work, consulting, speaking engagements, and crowdfunding. Diversification can enhance your financial stability.

- **Understand Media Economics:** Stay informed about changes in media economics, including advertising trends, subscription models, and philanthropic support for journalism.

9. Commit to Ethical Reporting

- **Fact-Checking:** Prioritize fact-checking and source verification to combat the spread of misinformation.

- **Transparency:** Maintain transparency in your reporting process, acknowledging any potential conflicts of interest.

10. Never Stop Learning

- **Professional Development:** Invest in ongoing learning through journalism courses, workshops, and online resources. Stay informed about industry trends and best practices.

- **Adaptability:** Be open to change and adapt quickly to new technologies and shifts in the media landscape.

The future of internet journalism holds limitless potential for those who are prepared to embrace the challenges and opportunities it presents. By combining strong journalistic fundamentals with technological proficiency and an unwavering commitment to ethics, you can position yourself as a resilient and influential internet journalist in the ever-evolving media ecosystem.

As you embark on your journey in internet journalism, remember that adaptability, curiosity, and a passion for truth are your most valuable assets. With these qualities and a dedication to lifelong learning, you'll be well-equipped to make a meaningful impact in the rapidly changing field of digital journalism.

Chapter 13: Professional Organizations and Associations

Professional organizations and associations play a vital role in supporting and advancing the interests of internet journalists. These groups provide networking opportunities, resources, and a sense of community for journalists working in the digital sphere. Here are some prominent organizations and associations that cater to professionals in internet journalism:

1. Online News Association (ONA)

- **Overview:** ONA is a leading organization dedicated to inspiring and supporting innovation in digital journalism. It brings together journalists, editors, technologists, and educators to foster a vibrant digital news ecosystem.

- **Membership Benefits:** ONA offers access to conferences, webinars, workshops, and a global network of journalists. Members can stay updated on industry trends and best practices.

2. International Consortium of Investigative Journalists (ICIJ)

- **Overview:** ICIJ is renowned for its investigative reporting on global issues. It's a network of journalists and media organizations that collaborate on in-depth investigations, often involving data journalism and cross-border reporting.

- **Membership Benefits:** ICIJ provides access to exclusive investigations, data tools, and resources for journalists interested in investigative reporting.

3. Association for Data Journalism and Digital Storytelling (DJA)

- **Overview:** DJA focuses on the intersection of data journalism and digital storytelling. It supports journalists who work with data, visualizations, and interactive storytelling.

- **Membership Benefits:** Members gain access to conferences, webinars, and resources for data-driven reporting and multimedia storytelling.

4. Society of Professional Journalists (SPJ)

- **Overview:** SPJ is one of the oldest and most respected journalism organizations in the United States. While it encompasses journalism in various forms, it offers resources and support for digital journalists.

- **Membership Benefits:** SPJ provides networking opportunities, training sessions, legal support, and advocacy for journalists.

5. Digital Journalism Task Force (DJTF)

- **Overview:** Part of the National Association of Black Journalists (NABJ), DJTF focuses on issues related to digital journalism. It aims to promote diversity and inclusion in the digital media landscape.

- **Membership Benefits:** Members can access webinars, networking events, and resources that promote diversity and representation in digital journalism.

6. Association of Health Care Journalists (AHCJ)

- **Overview:** AHCJ caters to journalists covering health-related topics, including those in the digital space. It offers resources for investigative health reporting in the digital age.

- **Membership Benefits:** AHCJ provides access to health data, conferences, training, and connections with experts in the healthcare field.

7. Investigative Reporters and Editors (IRE)

- **Overview:** IRE is dedicated to supporting investigative journalism. While it encompasses various forms of journalism, it offers valuable resources for digital journalists engaged in investigative reporting.

- **Membership Benefits:** Members gain access to investigative reporting tools, data sets, training, and an extensive network of investigative journalists.

8. The Media Consortium

- **Overview:** The Media Consortium is a network of progressive, independent media organizations. It supports journalists and outlets that produce digital content with a focus on social justice and equity.

- **Membership Benefits:** The consortium offers opportunities for collaboration, grants, and resources for independent digital journalists.

Joining a professional organization or association in internet journalism can provide numerous advantages, including access to valuable resources, networking opportunities, and a platform to advocate for the industry's interests. As the field continues to evolve, these organizations play a pivotal role in shaping the future of journalism in the digital age.

Glossary of Internet Journalism Terms

1. Clickbait
- **Definition:** Clickbait refers to sensational or misleading headlines and content designed to entice users to click on a link or visit a website, often for the purpose of generating advertising revenue.

2. Content Management System (CMS)
- **Definition:** A CMS is a software platform used by news organizations to create, publish, and manage digital content. It allows journalists to update websites and publish articles without needing extensive technical knowledge.

3. User-Generated Content (UGC)
- **Definition:** UGC refers to content created and contributed by users, often in the form of comments, photos, videos, or social media posts. News outlets may incorporate UGC into their reporting.

4. Paywall
- **Definition:** A paywall is a barrier that restricts access to certain online content, typically requiring users to pay a subscription fee or make a one-time payment to access premium articles or features.

5. SEO (Search Engine Optimization)
- **Definition:** SEO is the practice of optimizing online content to rank higher in search engine results.

Journalists use SEO techniques to increase the visibility of their articles on search engines like Google.

6. Hyperlink

- **Definition:** A hyperlink, often referred to as a link, is a clickable element that connects one web page to another or to a different part of the same page. Hyperlinks are used extensively in online journalism to provide references and sources.

7. Algorithm

- **Definition:** An algorithm is a set of rules or instructions used by search engines and social media platforms to determine the order and visibility of content in users' feeds or search results.

8. Viral

- **Definition:** When content spreads rapidly and widely across the internet, it is said to have gone viral. Viral content often gains massive attention and shares on social media.

9. Livestreaming

- **Definition:** Livestreaming involves broadcasting real-time video or audio content over the internet. Journalists use livestreams to cover breaking news events and engage with their audience in real-time.

10. Analytics

- **Definition:** Analytics tools provide data and insights about website traffic, user behavior, and content performance. Journalists use analytics to evaluate the success of their articles and make data-driven decisions.

11. Troll

- **Definition:** A troll is an individual who deliberately posts inflammatory, offensive, or disruptive comments or messages online, often with the intention of provoking others or derailing discussions.

12. Blogging

- **Definition:** Blogging involves writing and publishing articles, opinions, or commentary on a personal or organizational website. Blogs are a common format for opinion pieces and niche journalism.

13. Podcast

- **Definition:** A podcast is an audio program available for streaming or download on the internet. Journalists use podcasts to discuss news, share interviews, and provide in-depth analysis.

14. Aggregator

- **Definition:** An aggregator is a website or platform that collects and compiles news articles and content from various sources, presenting them in one location for users to access.

15. Engagement

- **Definition:** Engagement in internet journalism refers to the level of interaction and participation of readers with online content. This includes actions like commenting, sharing, and liking articles.

16. Curation

- **Definition:** Content curation involves the selection and organization of online content from various sources to create a cohesive narrative or collection of information on a specific topic.

17. Influencer

- **Definition:** An influencer is an individual with a significant online following and the ability to shape opinions and trends. Some journalists collaborate with influencers to promote their content.

18. Embed

- **Definition:** To embed is to insert media (such as videos, tweets, or maps) from one website or platform into another, allowing readers to view the content without leaving the page.

19. Geolocation

- **Definition:** Geolocation involves identifying and tagging the location of a news event or user-generated content, often using GPS or metadata from photos and videos.

20. Real-Time Reporting

- **Definition:** Real-time reporting involves delivering news updates and information as events unfold. Journalists use social media and live coverage to provide immediate updates.

Style Guide for Online Journalism

A style guide for online journalism is a crucial resource that ensures consistency, clarity, and professionalism in digital reporting. It provides guidelines for writers, editors, and content creators to follow when producing online content. Here, we delve into the key components of an effective style guide for Internet journalism.

1. Writing Style and Tone

- **Objective Language:** Encourage the use of clear and objective language in reporting. Avoid sensationalism and biased language.

- **Conversational Tone:** Online journalism often adopts a conversational tone to engage readers. Specify when and how to use this tone appropriately.

2. Headlines and Subheadings

- **Headline Length:** Set limits on headline length for readability and SEO optimization.

- **Clarity:** Emphasize the importance of clear and informative headlines that accurately represent the content.

3. SEO Guidelines

- **Keyword Usage:** Instruct writers on how to incorporate relevant keywords naturally into content to improve search engine visibility.

- **Meta Tags:** Explain the significance of meta titles and descriptions in driving organic traffic.

4. Attribution and Sourcing

- **Citing Sources:** Establish guidelines for proper source attribution and citation, emphasizing the importance of verifying and crediting information.

- **Hyperlinking:** Explain when and how to include hyperlinks to external sources, supporting transparency and additional context.

5. Formatting and Multimedia

- **Text Formatting:** Define text formatting rules, such as bold, italics, and bullet points, for consistency.

- **Multimedia Integration:** Instruct on how to incorporate images, videos, infographics, and other multimedia elements effectively.

6. Ethical Guidelines

- **Plagiarism:** Explicitly state the consequences of plagiarism and stress the importance of original reporting and proper attribution.

- **Privacy and Consent:** Address ethical considerations related to privacy, consent, and the use of sensitive information.

7. Social Media and Engagement

- **Social Sharing:** Provide guidance on creating compelling social media posts to promote articles and engage with readers.

- **Interactivity:** Encourage audience engagement through comments, polls, and interactive elements.

8. Accessibility

- **Web Accessibility:** Highlight the importance of making content accessible to all readers, including those with disabilities. Address techniques for alt text, captions, and readable fonts.

9. Legal Considerations

- **Copyright:** Explain copyright laws and fair use principles, along with the proper way to use copyrighted material.

- **Defamation:** Address legal risks related to defamation and libel, emphasizing fact-checking and responsible reporting.

10. Updates and Corrections

- **Correction Policy:** Outline a clear process for handling errors and corrections, ensuring transparency and accountability.

- **Timestamps:** Specify when and how to update articles and provide timestamps for revisions.

11. Mobile Optimization

- **Responsive Design:** Stress the importance of designing content for mobile devices to accommodate a mobile-first audience.

12. Analytics and Metrics

- **Traffic Monitoring:** Explain how to interpret website analytics and metrics to gauge the performance of articles.

- **Audience Insights:** Encourage the use of data to understand audience preferences and tailor content accordingly.

13. Engagement and Moderation Guidelines

- **Community Guidelines:** Establish rules for user engagement and comment moderation to maintain a respectful and constructive online community.

- **Troll Management:** Offer strategies for dealing with online trolls and disruptive behavior.

14. Emergencies and Crisis Reporting

- **Breaking News:** Define procedures for reporting breaking news events responsibly and ethically.

- **Verification:** Stress the importance of verifying information before publishing during emergencies.

A well-crafted style guide serves as a foundational document that empowers journalists and content creators to produce high-quality, reliable, and engaging online journalism. It ensures that digital reporting aligns with the principles of accuracy, transparency, and ethical conduct while adapting to the dynamic nature of the internet. Consistently following the style guide fosters trust with readers and enhances the overall quality of online journalism.

This style guide for online journalism covers essential aspects of digital reporting, including writing style, SEO, ethical considerations, multimedia integration, and more. It provides a comprehensive framework for journalists to produce content that is informative, engaging, and in alignment with journalistic standards

Sample Online Newsroom Policies and Guidelines

1. Mission Statement

- **Mission:** Our online newsroom is committed to providing accurate, timely, and reliable information to our audience. We prioritize journalistic integrity, ethical reporting, and transparency in all our content.

2. Editorial Standards

- **Accuracy:** Accuracy is paramount. All information must be fact-checked and verified before publication. Editors and reporters are responsible for ensuring the correctness of their content.

- **Fairness and Objectivity:** We present news in a fair, unbiased, and objective manner. Avoid any form of discrimination, bias, or prejudice in reporting.

- **Transparency:** Clearly attribute sources, disclose potential conflicts of interest, and provide context to help readers understand the full story.

3. Content Creation and Publishing

- **Original Reporting:** We prioritize original reporting and discourage the use of unverified or uncredited content.

- **Citing Sources:** Properly attribute and cite sources. Hyperlink to external sources when referencing their content.

- **Headlines and Subheadings:** Craft clear, informative, and accurate headlines and subheadings that reflect the content of the article.

4. Multimedia Integration

- **Images and Videos:** Use images and videos responsibly, ensuring that they are relevant, accurate, and properly credited.

- **Alt Text:** Provide alt text for images to make content accessible to readers with disabilities.

5. Engagement and Moderation

- **Comment Moderation:** Moderators must maintain a respectful and constructive comment section. Remove spam, hate speech, and abusive comments promptly.

- **Social Media Engagement:** Engage with the audience on social media platforms respectfully and professionally. Respond to inquiries and feedback.

6. Ethical Considerations

- **Plagiarism:** Plagiarism is strictly prohibited. All content must be original or properly attributed.

- **Privacy and Consent:** Respect individuals' privacy rights and obtain proper consent for using personal information or images.

- **Sensationalism:** Avoid sensationalized or misleading content for the purpose of clicks or views.

7. Corrections and Updates

- **Corrections:** Acknowledge and correct errors transparently. Include a correction note at the end of the article.

- **Updates:** Clearly indicate when an article has been updated and provide timestamps for revisions.

8. Social Media and SEO

- **Social Media Guidelines:** Follow guidelines for social media usage, including sharing content and engaging with the audience.

- **SEO Best Practices:** Optimize content for search engines by incorporating relevant keywords and meta descriptions.

9. Accessibility

- **Web Accessibility:** Ensure that all online content is accessible to readers with disabilities. Use readable fonts and proper formatting.

10. Data Security

- **Protection of Sources:** Safeguard the identities and information of confidential sources, complying with legal protections for journalists.

- **Data Privacy:** Adhere to data privacy laws when collecting and handling user data.

11. Emergency Reporting

- **Breaking News:** Follow established procedures for reporting breaking news events responsibly and ethically.

- **Verification:** Verify information rigorously during emergency reporting to avoid spreading misinformation.

12. Legal and Copyright

- **Copyright Compliance:** Respect copyright laws and obtain necessary permissions for using copyrighted material.

- **Legal Consultation:** Seek legal counsel in case of potential legal disputes or challenges.

13. Review and Accountability

- **Regular Review:** Periodically review and update these guidelines to ensure relevance and compliance with evolving journalistic standards.

- **Accountability:** All staff members, including freelancers and contributors, are accountable for adhering to these guidelines. Violations may result in disciplinary action.

14. Training and Education

- **Training:** Provide training and resources for staff on journalistic ethics, online security, and digital tools.

- **Continuing Education:** Encourage staff to engage in continuous learning and professional development.

These sample online newsroom policies and guidelines serve as a framework for maintaining journalistic integrity and ethical standards in digital reporting. News organizations can adapt and customize these guidelines to align with their specific editorial missions and values. Consistently upholding these principles contributes to trustworthy and responsible journalism in the digital age.

These policies and guidelines are designed to ensure the ethical, accurate, and responsible reporting of news in the digital realm. News organizations can use this sample as a starting point to create their own tailored set of policies and guidelines that reflect their unique mission and values.

Conclusion

In the ever-evolving landscape of journalism, the internet has emerged as both a challenge and an opportunity. Internet journalism has redefined the way news is gathered, presented, and consumed. It has shattered the boundaries of traditional media, giving rise to a global network of citizen journalists, bloggers, and digital news organizations. As we conclude our exploration of this dynamic field, several key themes and takeaways come to the forefront:

1. **The Digital Evolution of Journalism:** We have witnessed the transformation of journalism in the digital age. The internet has brought speed and accessibility to news reporting, enabling real-time updates and global reach. It has democratized information dissemination, allowing diverse voices to contribute to the news ecosystem.

2. **Ethical Imperatives:** As we navigate the digital realm, ethical considerations remain paramount. The principles of accuracy, fairness, and transparency are as vital as ever. Internet journalists must grapple with issues like fake news, misinformation, and the responsible use of user-generated content.

3. **Technological Advancements:** The tools and technologies available to internet journalists continue to evolve. From data analytics to multimedia

storytelling, these innovations empower journalists to engage audiences in new and compelling ways.

4. **Engagement and Community Building:** Internet journalism extends beyond news reporting; it fosters engagement and community. Journalists must actively participate in online conversations, responding to readers' comments and concerns. Building a strong online presence and nurturing an engaged audience are essential skills.

5. **Challenges and Opportunities:** Internet journalism faces challenges, from the monetization of online content to the need for digital security. However, these challenges also present opportunities for innovation, collaboration, and audience growth.

6. **The Future Awaits:** As we look ahead, the future of internet journalism is filled with promise. Emerging technologies like artificial intelligence and immersive storytelling are poised to reshape the field. The continued dedication to journalistic ethics and the pursuit of truth will remain guiding principles.

In closing, internet journalism is a dynamic and ever-changing realm where the pursuit of truth and the commitment to responsible reporting are unwavering. As technology advances and new platforms emerge, the essence of journalism—the search for facts, the telling of stories, and the fostering of an informed society—endures. Internet journalism stands as a testament to the enduring spirit of journalism itself, embracing the digital age while preserving the principles that have guided the profession for centuries.

We invite you, dear reader, to embark on your own journey within the realm of internet journalism, armed with knowledge, curiosity, and a commitment to ethical reporting. As the digital world continues to evolve, so too will the landscape of journalism. And in this evolution, we find the boundless potential to inform, inspire, and shape the future.

Thank you for joining us on this exploration of Internet Journalism. We look forward to the stories you will uncover, the insights you will share, and the positive impact you will make in this vibrant and ever-changing field.

About Author

Osman Karakas is an accomplished journalist, editor, researcher, photographer, and author with a diverse and extensive background in the field of journalism. With a passion for storytelling and a commitment to journalistic integrity, Osman Karakas has made significant contributions to the media industry throughout his career.

Osman Karakas has been recognized for his outstanding work and has received numerous awards and accolades. In 1991, he was honored with the Excellence in Journalism award by the Deadline Club-Society of Professional Journalists in New York, USA.

In 1990, Osman Karakas won first place in the Spot News category at the Associated Press Association, New York, for his impactful news story titled "Don't Let Him Die" published in the New York Post.

He also received the prestigious Picture of the Year Award in 1990 from the University of Missouri - School of Journalism/National Press Photographers Association, his photography was compared to Michelangelo's "Pieta" by the head of the jury.

His international experience continued as they worked as a correspondent at the United Nations for Anadolu Weekly in New York, USA, and later as a Correspondent and News & Photo Editor for Hurriyet International Daily, covering press conferences at the UN.

In addition to his international assignments, Osman Karakas his career in journalism as a correspondent for TRT (Turkish Radio & Television) in Turkmenistan and Kazakhstan from 1993 to 1996. During this time, they also served as the Editor-in-Chief of the TURKCAN International Magazine in Turkmenistan. Also manager and editor-in-Chief various newspapers and magazines in Türkiye and Central Asia.

Osman Karakas has been involved in academia as well, having worked as a Lecturer at Manas University in Bishkek, Kyrgyzstan, where they taught journalism courses, advised students, and served on various committees about 8 years. His dedication to education and knowledge sharing has been instrumental in nurturing the next generation of journalists.

With proficiency in multiple languages, including English, Turkish, Russian, Turkmen, Azerbaijan, Kyrgyz, and Kazakh, Osman Karakas has been able to communicate and report on diverse topics with cultural sensitivity and understanding. his language skills have allowed them to engage with various communities and provide insightful coverage.

Alongside his journalistic career, Osman Karakas has authored several books and documentaries, covering topics ranging from journalism to detective novels and documentaries on historical events. They have also exhibited his photography in multiple personal exhibitions in Turkey and Kyrgyzstan, showcasing his artistic talent and unique perspective.

Osman Karakas possesses a wide range of skills and expertise, including diplomacy, media relations, public relations, political campaign management, managing media, photography, communication, and web publishing. Including; advertising, social media, and desktop publishing, keeping up with the evolving landscape of digital journalism.

In conclusion, Osman Karakas has made significant contributions to the field of journalism through his exceptional work, awards, publications, and dedication to journalistic ethics. His diverse experiences, international exposure, and commitment to storytelling have shaped his career and established them as a respected figure in the media industry.

Recommended Books

The Complete Guide to
INVESTIGATIVE
JOURNALISM
A Handbook for Candidate and
New - Beginner Journalists
OSMAN KARAKAS
Award-winning Journalist & Lecturer

A COMPREHENSIVE AND
PRACTICAL GUIDEBOOK
News Writing
Techniques
MOST COMMON MISTAKES AND TIPS
OSMAN KARAKAS
AWARD-WINNING JOURNALIST & LECTURER

PROFESSIONAL
PHOTO
JOURNALISM
NEW YORK POST
'Don't let
him die!'
A Comprehensive Study Guide
for Professional Journalists
OSMAN KARAKAS
Award-winning Journalist & Lecturer

THE SOCIAL
MEDIA
PARADOX
Citizen Journalism or
Social Media Terror?
OSMAN KARAKAS
AWARD-WINNING JOURNALIST & LECTURER

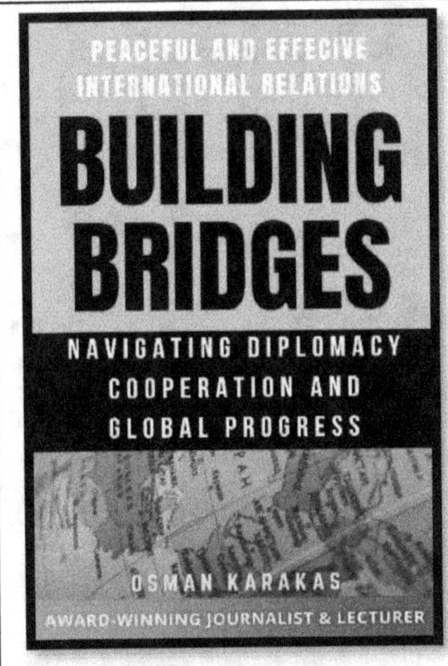
PEACEFUL AND EFFECIVE INTERNATIONAL RELATIONS
BUILDING BRIDGES
NAVIGATING DIPLOMACY COOPERATION AND GLOBAL PROGRESS
OSMAN KARAKAS
AWARD-WINNING JOURNALIST & LECTURER

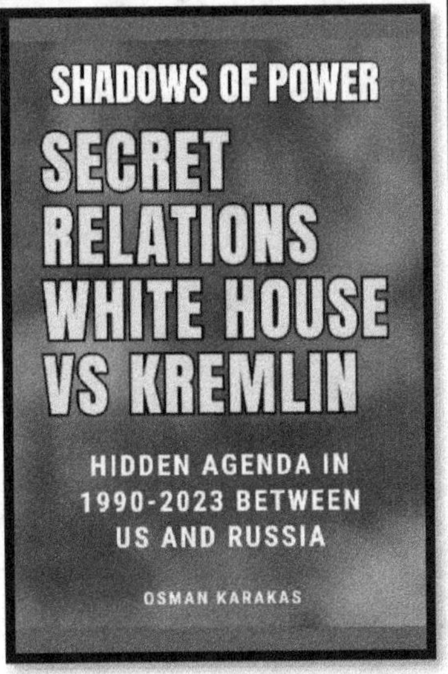
SHADOWS OF POWER
SECRET RELATIONS WHITE HOUSE VS KREMLIN
HIDDEN AGENDA IN 1990-2023 BETWEEN US AND RUSSIA
OSMAN KARAKAS

COMPREHENSIVE GUIDE THAT EXPLORES THE INTRICATE WORLD OF CRISIS DIPLOMACY
ART OF DIPLOMACY IN CRISES
NAVIGATING INTERNATIONAL RELATIONS WITH FINESSE AND STRATEGIC EXCELLENCE
OSMAN KARAKAS

Journalists Selling Their Pen in the Media World
EMBEDDED /JERKS
OSMAN KARAKAS
AWARD-WINNING JOURNALIST & LECTURER

THE DARK
UNDERBELLY
Unmasking the Secrets of
Entertainment Programs
Exposing Manipulation,
Scandals and the Price of Fame
in Show Business
OSMAN KARAKAS

MANIPULATION
OF MEDIA
NEWS
THE EROSION OF REALITY IN THE
MODERN NEWS LANDSCAPE
OSMAN KARAKAS
AWARD-WINNING JOURNALIST & LECTURER

INTERNATIONAL
JOURNALISM
Global Perspectives of
International News
OSMAN KARAKAS
AWARD-WINNING JOURNALIST & LECTURER

An Easy-to-Digest Exploration
of Africa's Complex Realities
The Dark
Destiny
of
AFRICA
Navigating Challenges, Forging Hope
OSMAN KARAKAS

The collection of books is accessible for purchase on Amazon.com platform.

www.ingramcontent.com/pod-product-compliance
Lightning Source LLC
Chambersburg PA
CBHW050808260726
48660CB00004B/1312